we don't have a compass but i'm sure we'll find home

r.i.d

First Printing: 2015

ISBN 978-1-312-76786-7

www.inkskinned.com

A NOTE FROM THE POET

All of the poems included in this book are written in response to anonymously submitted secrets. The quotations I include as titles are not my words, but rather what inspired the poem. My only hope has ever been that every person will see their story as valid. Without all of the support I get, I would be nothing. This book, and every poem in it: it was written for you, wherever you are, whatever you are doing. It was written because you deserve to have your secrets heard.

It was written because you are a poem, too, and it is effortless loving you.

everyone is so very
sad

and i know
i am no one
special

but i just want
to make them all
feel
better.

"I want to break off pieces of my happiness and hand them out to the whole world."

i never asked
for the waters
to be shallow nor
calm:
i only wanted
someone
to help me
swim along.

"I feel lost... I want someone who tells me that everything will be okay."

why would
you choose
me?

nobody else
ever
did.

"She tells me I'm her best friend, multiple times. I just don't believe her."

you cannot
hurt me

more than i
have hurt
myself
already.

"I wish I could tell my enemies: I hate myself more than you ever could."

---

how can i
be alive
when inside
it feels
as if
i have already
died?

"I taught myself not to feel anything... And now I've healed, but I still haven't found anything worth feeling."

i don't want a fancy dinner or
a hollywood date.

i want to eat
poorly-cooked pasta
while sitting on your counter
and laughing about
the faces you make.
i want to strip down
to my underwear
and watch bad action movies
with your body
beside me.
i want honey and i want
fries and i want
to not have to worry
about saying
goodbye.

"I'm just starting out this relationship and everything terrifying. I wish we could skip this whole dating part and just be together."

someone once asked her
what being
triggered
was like.

she closed her eyes
and thought
of planes crashing
and car accidents
but instead said

the beach,
falling asleep
under direct sun and laughter
only to wake up an hour after
suddenly drowning,
gargling salt water
where once had been air,
forgetting how to swim
and terrifyingly aware
that at that moment,
you could die,
right there.

"Lately I've been getting hit with strong waves of sadness that hit me at the most random times. I just don't know what's wrong with me."

where has
my childhood
gone?

did i leave it behind
on the
playground
one night?

all i remember is that

i used to like
life.

"I will never, ever be good enough. I'm in a constant battle with myself, and I never win."

i want to get into my car
and drive
until i find what i'm
looking for.
maybe it's a
purpose
or maybe it's
a new start
or maybe it's just
a sky
with unclouded
stars.

"I'm sick of this town, of my room, of my friends, and of myself. I want to leave so badly."

do i eat breakfast
or starve myself again?

tonight i will write
my suicide note,
but only in my head.

tomorrow i will wish
i was already dead,

and despite all this
i will still

get myself
out of bed.

"... I'll do anything not to gain a pound."

i think that i love
your flaws
maybe even more
than your perfections

because they're
proof to me
that you're real, that
you're human.

but our lips
almost knew each other

and that's what
kills me:

an almost-lover.

"I like him but he's over me. I feel so foolish for missing my chance and letting him slip through my fingers."

---

i cannot sleep
without your body
beside mine.

i don't know why
you chose me
but please,
please,
don't ever
leave.

no, you don't understand,
it's not that i don't try, it's that i try
so fucking *hard*
to be funny and smart and pretty and
deserving of your love

but despite every attempt
i'm still not
enough.

i just want to be
good
at something.

i want a talent
that makes me special.
i have such an addiction
to creation,
but everything i make
is always just

"not that great."

i have no reason
for relapse
at all

except that my skin
is no longer
scarred -

somehow,
that feels
so terribly
wrong.

"I've been thinking about cutting again."

at first the word *depression*
doesn't belong to you:
your mother writes off your self-destruction
as over-dramatic
since you're too young
to be broken
and besides,
what bad thing has even
happened to you
yet

you don't deserve a real diagnosis,
so you keep the condition under your skin,
wondering if
your apathy about everything
is just what all people
go through.

you don't want to be seen as
causing trouble again
so you sit down and shut up and decide
that you're absolutely fine,
you're just going through
a rough patch.
so what that one night
while babysitting the neighbors
you take a pair of scissors to the inside
of your left arm
and discover what being alive
is like.

you're not depressed, but you take to writing
wake up on the inside of your wrist
as if pleading with yourself
to find feeling again.

it's not an addiction even though
you come home from
a perfectly good day and
end up
cutting your skin
and only being able to sleep
when you're bleeding
again

but no,
you're young, you've got so much
to be grateful for
and such a bright future;
you're just battling
some unnamed giant
darkness

even though
there's no real way
out of this.

"I think I'm depressed."

no, i don't know why
i'm supposed to stay alive
when i can't even control
the size of my thighs

and they keep telling me
it gets better, don't worry
but when i blew out my candles,
i wished to be
as light as a feather

see but i have this
really excellent life
there's nothing to complain about
and no reason to cry

so why do i think about suicide
every single fucking
night?

i want to believe
that i'll be alright
but i can't shake the feeling
everyone would be better off
if i just had the courage
to finally
die.

_____

"What is the point?"

blue lips
and blue veins

soon i will be
cold
again

will you bury me
in a white dress fair?

when you bury me

will you care

peace and quiet
in graves so deep

this life is mine

to take
or
keep.

"I wrote a suicide note yesterday."

do not
hold my hand in public.
do not remember
my favorite kind of ice cream.
do not hum
when you run your fingers over my skin,
do not get me concert tickets, do not
kiss me when (i) am angry,
when i am crying, when i least
expect it. do not kiss me.
do not ask if i (will) go on adventures with you, do
not hold out a hand when i (fall) down, do not help me
back to my feet. do not read me your favorite books
to put me to sleep, do not talk to me (for) hours
on end, do not text me in the morning.
please, if you have any mercy,
do not make me love
(you).

"My favorite moment with him was kissing him in the rain."

i miss you,
do you know that?

everyone around me
is getting so much older
and their big beautiful lives
are picking up speed

so while they're off
in different countries,
kissing new people,
falling in love,
making art,
discussing space

i am slowly being
replaced.

"I'm on the verge of losing my best friend. It hurts."

the only person
you should ever worry about offending
is yourself,
six years from now.

if you think your tattoo will look radical
when you are twenty-seven,
get it and instagram the shit outta it.
use a nice filter.
be proud you know who you are
well enough to mark your body
to prove it
and if some poor fucker
judges you for that,
kick them hard enough they'll feel it later.

if you wanna make out with some random guy,
be open to what people tell you about him
and how he is,
but make your own choices. for instance,
if you're sure that cold sore is a little bit more,
maybe think twice. but if you know
the only reason you haven't
moved to smooch city
is because it'll *complicate* things,
uncomplicate that shit
with your lips.

if you wanna ride the roller coaster
but it looks like it could kill you,
get on that motherfucker.
eat the second bowl of ice cream.
call up your dad and tell him
you're sorry.

here's the thing:
do what feels right and in the future
you'll be happy

"This guy and I have fallen in love, but he's my ex's best friend. We don't know how to tell him..."

you don't
get it,
okay,

it's not easy
for me
to explain

but i'm not
trying to be
lazy, it's just
that i'm so
fucking
tired

and i have
no motivation
to succeed

and i don't even
know
why this life

is happening
to me.

"I used to be happy. I don't know what happened. Maybe it was high school."

in autumn i found a boy
who asked me to cut my hair
and said *i love you*
only after sex and six shots.
i sipped tea and told my friends about him
and they said *if you're happy* and
knew i was not.

in winter i kissed a girl
who tasted like cigarettes and said
i love you all the time
but hurt herself whenever i made mistakes.
she threatened to kill herself if ever i left.
my friends watched me wash my hands
and did not tell me to test that statement.

in spring i spent time with a boy
who told me it was his way or no way
and when i challenged that,
he told me
i love you and that's why i'm doing this.
my friends saw my bruises and gripped my wrists
while i said,
i deserve him.

in summer i wanted
no one at all
and when he walked into my life i didn't expect
to fall
but he kisses like the devil
while keeping all of my demons away.
my friends hold my gaze and tell me
keep him. stay.

"I didn't know what love was until I kissed him."

they will say *open up*
but when you do,
make sure you only talk about
small things that are easily solved.
talk about school, talk about feeling
left out sometimes.
never fucking mention
the thick blade lines.

do not trust them to text you back if you write
it's getting to be kind of a bad night.
instead add something like
i ate too much ice cream what woe is this
and then, when they turn away,
turn the razor to your wrist.

i know they have said you can ask for help at any time.
they mean with math homework,
not your demons.
when you send them a message that reads,
i'm thinking of taking pills right now,
make sure you save it somehow
with some lie or another like *what can stop*
this headache

because here's the thing
i'm sure you have guessed:

nobody knows how to save you from this.

"I put up walls and people ask me why I don't let them in. When I do, they run."

i. no, i am not scrolling through your words because I
   still love you,
   but instead because it's three a.m.
   and i am lonely and terrifically, terribly
   drunk.
ii. you once had me try
   each of the wines in your parent's basement stash.
   i couldn't tell them apart, but i liked
   pretending.
   it was nice, having you be only
   mine.
iii. once, on our third date,
   you got your hair caught in your zipper and your
   cheeks reddened and you grew so flustered
   you looked as if you were about to cry,
   but in all the time we were together,
   you never did.
iv. the place where you used to be is getting blistered
   because i keep running my fingers over it.
   maybe your smile was blinding
   or i was just
   ignorant.
v. the last text you sent
   still sounds like you love me
   but it's three a.m.
   and we'll never be
   us
   ever again.

---

*"I decided to reread the messages between my ex and me. I fell in love with her all
   over again."*

how many stars
can you count tight
by connecting your freckles
with pretty red lines?

it *burns* in the shower,
but that's okay.
you don't deserve to feel
happy
anyway.

you could be magical
but there's only one problem:
your demons run wild
and you have no idea
how to stop them.

you tug jeans over your hips
and make your thighs cry.

you still pray for an accident
so you could finally
die.

"They left me to my own devices, yet they were horrified when they found my wrists
    slashed."

i know better
but i still check your facebook
late at night,
finding the page before
i find the sense to turn away.

it's never easy,
seeing how happy you are with her.
in fairness, she's sweet, and all the times i've
talked with her,
i could really see why
you'd love her.
sometimes i scroll through
all of her photos,
wanting to hate her
and hating myself
for wanting that.

the way you look at her
is like
she is your anchor
in high-riding waves.

you never looked
at me
that way.

"I told him how I feel, but after months of pain, all I want is to be as close as we used to be..."

i.   insomnia, as diagnosed by a doctor who smells like old tobacco. when you tell your boyfriend, he inhales a cigarette and says *everyone has it.* your sheets are stained with sweat and you take pills that don't let you wake up from nightmares.

ii.   anxiety, first class, noticed when you started tearing with your teeth at the skin next to your fingertips. you are reading the medical report next to him when he says that he thinks anxiety is just your mind letting society in. you cannot breathe in movie theaters and spend concerts wondering which direction you would run in if someone came in with a gun. you knit your fingers and tightly together as you can so you do not hold him with your sweaty palms.

iii.   depression, diagnosed as *lazy* by your mother and *too tired* by your lover, a blanket term you're learning means wanting to swallow bleach and step in front of fast cars. you instead chase the bitter world with self-harm, blades in the places he should be holding you tighter; burn scars on the back of your thighs that he doesn't even notice, just fucks you without lights.

iv.   ednos; eating disorder, not otherwise specified. you're trapped between it being a real problem and finding your own solution, too scared to let it get to you but not strong enough to fight it off. he knows how close you are to the greatest relapse of your life and still plays with the fat on your body without thinking, pinching it to watch all the ripples spread. some part of you realizes he wouldn't even care if you wound up

v.   dead.

"I keep telling him about my mental illnesses but he doesn't seem to care."

you let him fuck you
because you were empty inside and
the tabloids were pills you felt like popping.

you wanted him to be rough, a bad poem, you wanted
to hurt in the morning. you wanted bruises on your
collarbones, empty lust,
nothing special.

instead he was urban exploration,
he ran all over your body as if each piece was hanging
in a museum,
he held you tight to him
and couldn't stop nibbling on your skin,
couldn't stop tracing patterns across your ribs in
invisible cartography, couldn't stop
treating you as if you were holy ground.

he didn't kiss you as he should have, he kissed you
like a prince
and that pissed you off

because,
god,
you never asked
to fall in love.

"It's funny because all he wanted was sex and I went along with it and now we are thinking about being in a relationship."

see, here's the truth:

either you are going to die
and leave the one you love
behind

or they're going to leave you
first.

nobody talks about that.

nobody talks about how
one way or another
everything ends

and there's nothing
you can do
about it.

"I don't know what to do. I'm miserable."

i'm sorry.

i know that you wanted me to be
everything i could
and instead i just chose
to be
broken.

it's just that i'm a kind of tired
that sleeping
doesn't cure.
i'm a kind of tired
that sits in your bones
and makes them too heavy
to carry
along

and it's just
that it's been like this
for as long
as i can remember:

everything inside of me shattering
while i try to hold it together.

"I do what needs to be done for me to be 'perfect.' I'm tired of it though."

compliments make you sick to your stomach
because they don't feel
good
anymore.

they feel like a swift punch
packaged in a lie

because whenever someone says,
you're beautiful

you hear,
i hate you, go die.

it is 2:51 on a thursday afternoon
and you could stain the rug
with your blood but
instead i want you to stain your hands
with paint or with ink or with oreo crumbs.
put the gun down.
go outside. find a farmer's market
or the produce section or
your garden. find a berry,
mash it between your teeth,
your fingers, your knees. get it in your hair,
get it on your sheets.

i love you,
so jump in the shower and wash off the bad things.
wash off all that you're covered in.
laugh at nothing.
scrub down, exfoliate,
moisturize, condition.
wrap a towel around yourself
or maybe just go naked through the streets.
eat ice cream or frozen yogurt or a banana.
save a dog from a shelter,
name him skippy,
sing him ballads while you're drunk.
write a novel. throw a party,
invite only yourself,
don't show up.

cover yourself in berries.

here's the thing: you should smear yourself
in every possible experience
before you step out of here.

but it's not going to fix just like that.

there's no magical cure.
it's going to hurt
and take time and
you'll fall down a lot.

but if you're already here, at the bottom:
you already know
how far you can fall
before you finally
stop.

"It's 2:51 on a Thursday afternoon and I have a gun in front of me, debating whether or not to put it up to my temple and pull the trigger."

do yourself a favor: if he is not going to love you,
stop loving him.

stop thinking about his smile while you rub shampoo
into your hair or while you slide soap down your
shinbones. only shave if it's what you prefer, not
because you hope that today might be the one he'll
notice you're attractive. stop wondering if he likes your
dress because it's more important that *you* like
your dress. stop taking mental notes while watching
bad romance movies, instead laugh and point out all
the plot holes and bad acting. stop cutting out pictures
of pretty girls from magazines to put up onto your
walls, instead clip pictures of your loved ones on every
surface that will hold them. stop stalling in the
hallways because you're trying to see him, and instead,
just go to class.

stop wondering what you're doing wrong, because
honestly,

you're doing everything fine, i promise. no, instead of
worrying about him and worrying about how to give
him the world:

instead, love yourself. that's the sort of love you
deserve.

"He may never love me."

last night
when your friend of eleven years was
five minutes late to picking you up,
you spent the whole time wondering
if she had secretly made plans to ditch you.
you knew that she had never done it before
and it would be out of character for her
but you couldn't get past
what a great joke it would be
if they all convinced you that you were invited
and then left you at home to later see
the facebook pictures of all the fun
they had without you.

you love your boyfriend
and that's supposed to come
with one hundred percent trust
but you still accidentally time
how long it takes him to text you back,
not because you hate that he's busy
but because when a message has gone read but
not replied to,
you start assuming
that you're annoying him
and he would be better off
without you.

you don't even think your family loves you,
rather they're putting up with you because
they have to –
no, if there's one thing
you actually *trust*,

it's that even though they all say they like you,
nobody really does.

"I don't understand how to trust people."

the only things made up in this poem are the names.

i am the teacher of twenty-four beautiful kids and in
between two lessons, i overhear maddie telling her
friend that jeremy is nice but they aren't going to talk
to him because he's fat and fat is bad. by the time i
have found words again, we are halfway through math.

jeremy sits in the back of the class and gives the girl
who forgot her snack half of his, and even though our
rule is that we never share food, i pretend not to see it.
maddie won't finish her meal. she tells me she's already
eaten too much, even though she only had
nine crackers for lunch.

i picture her stick-thin mother who
has collarbones like i would die for,
ribs jutting out like dinosaur claws on either side of a
slim body, slowly teaching maddie that teeth and
tongues are only for speaking, never for eating.
i picture jeremy growing up sad, searching for
something he can't put his finger on.
i give jeremy a free pencil when no one is looking, i
tell him that if something goes wrong, that if he's ever
hurt or angry or afraid, he can come talk to me,
he says he's afraid that something is wrong with
maddie.

the thing is, this sounds like your typical story
of teenage self-doubt, a girl who is struggling with
all those issues society talks about while shoving
body-image problems down her throat in place of
nutrition, it sounds like just the way the world works in
junior high

but i teach preschool.
jeremy is four and maddie is five.

"Sometimes I think I'm beautiful, but as soon as I see the rest of my body..."

i wonder if you hate father's day
since it would remind you
of what you gave up or,
hey, maybe
you love it
because it no longer reminds you
of us.

i wonder if you wonder about me or
out there in the world you just
are content in assuming that i'm doing okay.
i wonder if you write me letters that you are
too scared to send
because i have ninety-four postcards
that would show up at your door
if i only knew where to address them.

i wonder if you care about
what you created
or maybe hated the idea that
you'd watch me grow up
and see you own face
reflected.

I know other people have it worse, but I just wish my mom could be with him."

i want to go back in time and
find myself at fifteen. there's one minute
in particular where i remember
being balanced on the edge of recovery
and one of the worst relapses i had
ever considered

i remember sitting there with a blade between
my shaking fingers, trying to decide
if i really had any reason to survive,
thinking to myself *i need someone to hold me*.
i did not think to wrap my arms around my own body.

i want to take that little half-broken girl
and fold her against my chest, i want to let her cry
until her insides are raw and her eyes run dry.
i want to kiss her hair and say *look at me* and
let her take in the girl that she'll be
because we are never perfect but
we stop thinking perfection
is how we are supposed to be.

i want to read her writing with a kind heart
because i know that no matter where she turned,
people put down her notebooks before they finished
the stories. i want to give her pictures of the friends
we've made; show her the world she'll grow up
to see. i want to tell her, *you will learn to love,
but for right now, just be.*

if you are fifteen and wishing you could
just stop existing: here is a note from yourself
at twenty:
it works out. we are happy.
keep going.

"I'm finally okay."

every person is fighting a war inside the battlefield
of their ribs. the ground gets
so pliant when it's covered
in blood. maybe that's why the ones who are wounded
are the softest to touch.

i know people who are
painting targets on their cheekbones
while refusing to return fire.
i know people who are
swallowing harsh words like wasp nests
and still remembering to smile.
i know people who feel so broken that
they handle every stranger gently, out of fear
of making a similar hole -
i find those dealing with the most
are usually the ones to offer help
first.

i believe,
despite everything,
this world is filled with
more beauty than cruelty.
i know that evil shouts so loudly
that it has drowned you in
hopelessness.
but look for the ones
with flowers in their fingers, who kiss
instead of making fists.

one day, i promise.
you'll find that good exists.

"The world would be so much better if everybody just loved twice as much as they hated."

i just feel like shit.

this morning i woke up and stared at the wall
and told myself:
get out of bed.
shower.
your day can't start like this.

but i just lay there, bones suddenly brick,
knowing i'd have to rush and
it would be a bad day if i did
and not being able to move a single
fucking
inch.

get up, i said. *do something.*
you can't be like this.
get up. get out of bed, you piece
of shit.

but i couldn't. i couldn't.

"I don't know what I'm sorry for, but I'm sorry."

my doctor once asked why i always keep my hands
clasped. i told her that they felt comfortable like that,
locked like treasure chests as tight as i can get them

but really it's because if i let them hang loose,
you can see how the anxiety shakes them.

last night a boy and i were talking about the
riskiest things we'd ever done. he was drunk.
he started speaking about the time he
almost committed suicide and
instead of rolling up my sleeves and
telling him that he wasn't alone
i begged him to stop talking. i said it was a secret
too sad to know.

my therapist thinks i am making
excellent progress.

the only thing i've gotten better at lately
is making it look like i'm
really okay.

"I am afraid to ask my therapist for help. I feel like a burden to everyone."

i want to write *leave me alone* on my forehead
and curl up in the furthest corner of my bed.

i can't handle people. i can't handle the idea of anyone
crying once i am gone. i can't handle
hurting someone else in my fall.

he keeps hitting walls trying to save me
because there is only blankness where there used to be
such brightness.

i have stopped talking because there's nothing
left to say.

i tell him, *i am too apathetic to give a fuck*
about anything anymore, so honest that by the time
the words are out of my throat, they are
nothing but whispers.

he holds my hand. he knows about the scars. he knows
some part of me is screaming
but it's so little,
so far.

"I self-harmed a few days ago. The first time in a while, and it was worse than usual."

i cried a lot last night
and you weren't there
to hold me.

your hair liked to stick up in the front and
when you told a dirty joke you'd
give me this little knowing smirk
while you waited for my reaction.

sometimes when i kissed you,
our teeth would click
because one of us would be
smiling too hard to focus.

the first time i knew you were leaving me
was when my socks didn't match and
instead of making a comment and nibbling
my collarbone like usual, you just said
why don't you have your shoes on.

they say that a clean break is cruel but
what's worse is watching
the light of his love
fade from his irises.
you start snatching at every moment
that passes, start forcing yourself
into perfection. it doesn't work
and his eyes stray
to other girls.

i wish it hadn't changed. i hate the way you spit
my name. i miss holding you on park benches
and dancing in the rain. i wish i believed
this could go back and be the same.

"I knew it from the moment I smelled smoke on his breath..."

i don't know, maybe it's kind of silly
but even just getting a text from you
makes every part of me
glow.

i want to tell the world how lucky i am, but
then again, if i show you off,
someone more deserving
might snatch you up.

sometimes i picture you meeting my friends and
falling in love with how much better than me
they all are. you belong with someone
who can hold her liquor and can
actually dance and who has
never flunked a test.

but since you seem to have settled for me,
i promise i will not stop thanking you for it in
every small way that i can think of
because you might not be my whole life but
it certainly has been better ever since
you arrived.

so i swear i'll take the spiders outside
and wear your favorite dress every sunday and laugh at
your bad jokes and tuck you in and tell you stories and
take care of you when you're sick or hurting
and one day

if you want to,

i'll wait at the alter
just for you.

"He is my best friend. I think I want to spend the rest of my life with him."

i want to explain to the boy i love
that i have measured his spine with my fingertips
and it has always been the exact right length
to curl up beside
but when i say *i love you,*
he says, *why*

his father said little boys don't get to be sad
so my best friend started chewing down his emotions
in little acid tabs. he is broad fists and so guarded
that sometimes, even i'm not sure if he knows
how to let love in.

when he is angry, his fingers
pick up sharp things. he says the pain remains him
he's still human.

i am the black box of airplanes, a rolling tally
of screaming names. he used to curl his toes
around the edges of bridges and ask me what i'd do
if he jumped.

the thing is, when people are ready to go, they start
making jokes, just to see your reaction.
i didn't know that back then.

he kissed me once at a movie theater and said
i'm so sorry and couldn't say why.

they say depression is a girl's disease, that it's
an overemotional weakness.
i have been picking up the pieces
of little boys who blew their brains out
since i was in the second grade.
i cannot wash their sadness out of these walls. it
has stained them in tobacco bleakness.

a little while ago, someone i hadn't spoken to

for six years
reached out to me and said,
i just wanted to say goodbye before i leave.

i just wish i was a good enough poet to explain
how much every life
means.

"I'm thinking about suicide more and more."

the first time someone left me,
i read books where girls would position themselves
like sparrows, their long arms
balanced beautifully on windowpanes,
waiting for the return of their loved one.
i told myself i was too strong to keep a perpetual
lookout. i said, *the days are empty enough*

the third time someone left me,
it was my best friend. he said, *i hate you,*
and i said, *i understand.*
i told myself that there were other people out there
who wanted to keep me
maybe if not for any other reason
than being kept for decency.

the ninth time someone left me,
i learned there is a large difference between
someone dying and someone leaving.
i learned this in a graveyard while
grass clung to my feet.
maybe i was one of those people
who get a taste of death
and can't stop chasing it afterward.

i have stopped counting now.
people fall in snowflakes from my fingers
and i still do not perch in windows.
instead i fold myself into dark rooms and
try to nurse a wound that does not bleed.

the boy i love
asks why i hate being cold
and i do not tell him
that when you are left behind, there are
no more feelings.
you've been dropped in the tundra,
and it is freezing.

"The people that I love always leave me. And they just look so happy after that."

i no longer remember
what my skin looked like before the scars

some part of me wonders what
my children will say
when they see what i have done
but more of me wonders
if i'll even live that long

and how can i, in good faith, bring a person
into this world
knowing that they will inherit my desire
for self-destruction?
how would i be able to watch them wake up numb,
over and over? what if - god forbid - they are
less cowardly than i am
and they manage to actually
complete the deed?

i am so old and so young at the same time. i am
empty of heart but so full of self-hatred and
it is accumulating like layers of snow
under my skin.

soon i will be completely shut in.

"I have to change in the bathroom so they don't see my cuts."

please, for the love of god, do not tell
you look healthy.

it's weird how it takes you over.
people just roll their eyes and wonder aloud,
why don't you just eat?
but the thing is: at first you do. at first you're on
a normal diet and just cutting back on carbs
because you want to lose little around your middle, but
there comes a day when you figure that
there's no point in eating lunch anymore, not really,
and then you realize you function on just a cup of
black tea in the morning and then
the argument comes into your head that you don't need
food, not really, not when you'll only be hungry again
later - and suddenly it all gets tangled up and confusing
because you are only proud when you're empty
and being full makes you feel sick and you have
these dreams where you can eat anything again and
you wake up and you feel like crying from them and
there's so much pain you can't explain because, despite
constant starvation,
you're still not losing weight

so maybe i look healthy

but that doesn't mean i am
in any
way.

"They don't know that I hate my current body and am slowly working towards my
  past one."

if i wake up and do not remember who i am,
please, if you're kind,
do not tell me.

when i look down to this body and
ask why there are more scars than freckles,
lie.

do not bring up the blades.
let my addiction die.

make up a story about my childhood.
when i ask why food won't settle in my stomach,
please don't tell me about how i ruined
my own metabolism. instead just bring me to bed
and give me a past that is as edited as possible.
do not tell me the names of the people who left. do not
warn me about my flaws. let me
start over.

if i wake up and i no longer want to self-destruct,
please. do not remind me of who i was.
let me finally learn
to love.

_____

"He left me because of the scars on my arm."

a list of heavy things:

i. your backpack on the first day of school
where you wrap your fingers around the straps
and try to sit as quietly in class as possible
so as to go invisible.
ii. the lunch your mother made you at six in the morning,
and the sound it makes as it drops into a trashcan,
completely untouched.
you tell yourself the guilt is worth it.
iii. words like *fat* and *useless* as they settle on your
shoulders like carrion birds,
pecking at your skin and pulling on your
collarbones. they keep up their racket
into the long night when all others are asleep.
you keep your hands on your stomach
as you try to protect yourself
from their beaks.
iv. your smile. each day it gets a little bit harder
to lift the corners of your lips
convincingly.
v. the soul you carry, filled with debris and pollution,
bottles of liquor and razor blades and pills
all colliding in your veins.
vi. having to say *i'm fine*
every
single
day.

"I dreamed of suicide but the awakening to reality was what scared me."

all i can think of is how you would feel
lying in bed next to me or
finding your clothing tangled in mine when
i get up to do laundry.

i want a night as dark as chimneys to curl up in warm
blankets and read books while your fingertips
slowly etch out novels on my hipbones,
i want days as bright as sun off new snow,
to bundle up in four coats and go sledding with
no skill and end up half wet and all laughter and
fully out of breath. i want iced tea summers with
condensation on our glasses and fireflies between
our fingers and i want pumpkin spiced autumns
with leaf piles and halloween hauntings, i want to
reach out and know that your hand will find mine
even if i do it blindly, i want to lead you
over towns and countries and
through alleyways and mountains and under the stars

because where i belong
is wherever you are.

"Her laughter sounds like happiness. And I just want to spend the rest of my life lost in her eyes."

i got a great joke. what do you call a girl
who has tacked a *vacancy* sign to the insides
of her ribcage because whenever she breathes
she does not feel the rattle of her soul but rather
the expansion of a great sadness that has
completely taken over her
everything?

you call her a ghost, yeah, a
ghost.

okay, okay, stop me if you've heard this one.
anxiety, starvation, and self-hatred all walk
into the body of a person and they each
start to drink up every last scrap of hope
in the whole building. the punchline is that
eventually they end up burning down everything.

so this one is *really* hilarious. a boy who's
too tired to get out of bed
pretends to be happy literally every moment
because he doesn't want to be such a
huge fucking burden.
the scars on him look like white ivy and he thinks
only about suicide at the shutting of the night.
see, it's great because everybody thinks
he's doing alright.

see, it's funny, because in reality
we all want to die.

"They say I'm growing smaller every day. I wish I was around to notice."

you are every character i have ever written, you are
the paint on my canvas and the lyrics of my
music, you are the warmth of fleece blankets and
the bruises on my knees and the light in my
laughter

you are sitting across from me and grinning
and all i can think is how i could tell you at
this very moment that every love poem
i have read aloud to you
was my way of confessing,
that every book was just a valentine
someone else wrote

but then i picture this perfection
falling apart between my fingertips
only because i made things awkward by
confessing

and i wind up just saying
nothing.

"You are everything I've ever wanted and more. Please love me back."

when i was little i wasn't allowed to touch glass
because i kept breaking each beautiful thing
i could put my little hands on

i am older now and i haven't yet
gotten better at holding things
because i'm shaky like an old car
and i come apart easily

i break hearts and bones and bitter promises.
even i don't really know
what the next thing i fuck up
is going to be.

but i do know that
i am not safe to be around.
that's why i don't let people
close to me.

"I broke my best friend's heart. I didn't mean to."

i thank god every day
that i was too scared to kill myself.

i started spiraling at thirteen and by seventeen, i
was so bad that i thought i would never live to be thirty
and i burned out my body like a roman candle,
hated myself for not just
ending it all, but

it turns out that the small, terrified place of my brain
was just enough to save me
and i am so fucking grateful because without that one
little part that kept winning out,
i would have never met the boy i love, never
seen my favorite band in concert, never been
ice skating in total darkness or gone skinny dipping
or tried absinthe or made my own mozzarella sticks,
never would have heard so many songs that are now
my anthem, never would have learned to
love myself gently

and every time i fell down and scraped knees or
sobbed over my own soul, that little part said
get up, keep going
and at first i thought i was never going to be strong
enough, but if you do something enough times,
you get good at it,

and that little voice
became a deafening roar, so loud now that
when i'm starting to crumble, all i hear is
get up, keep going

i might not be perfect,
but i'm thriving, i'm growing.

"I'm too scared to commit suicide. So now I'm just stuck."

i once had a friend who liked to kick her heels off the
edge of the bridge over the train tracks and would
count the cars as they passed by underneath and since i
was too afraid of heights to be with her, she'd tell me
that today's number was eighty, sixteen, forty, three.
in exchange, i used to tell her tiny stories about my
day, about how i saw a leaf
i thought was looking for god or how i pet a dog
with a favorite food of overripe potatoes.

kids get old and the friends that were forever whittle
down into four-sentence text messages
and despite our best efforts, we grew apart,
except that every so often i'd get a text that said
twenty-eight today or i'd send her one that said
i have touched fire and thus felt eternity

i watched the light go out of her eyes. it was like
watching someone undress in total darkness. she
looked so sad and wore long sleeves all the time and
stopped coming to school as often. i picked up the
pace, sent her stories every day, just because
i couldn't figure out how else to help her.
she'd say *five, twelve, thirty.*

in the late night i got a call from her and she was
crying so hard i couldn't understand exactly what she
was saying and i ran so fast i forgot my balance and
kept skinning my knees but just getting up because i
knew i couldn't stop

i was in my pajamas and nothing else, standing on her
front lawn and begging her to let me in and

she opened the door with red wrists and stood there
with tears on her cheeks and said,

it was a bad day, one hundred eleven

i was all out of words so i took her into my arms and
counted out all of her scars,
the real count she'd been keeping
since she was old enough to hear them whisper,
one for each word they had buried her under and i
swore to take care of her from that moment on,
even if i was scared of the places she'd gone.

i kissed the top of her forehead and wrapped her arms
up and told her a story of a little girl
i'd always loved.

i hope one day my friendship will actually be enough.

"Sometimes everything is just too much and I feel like I'm coming out of my skin."

he's the kind of boy who will go out of his way
to find you mistletoe just because you mentioned once
that you've never had one of those kisses,
he's the kind of boy who will agree to balance reese's
peanut butter cups in between his teeth, just so you
make a game out of eating the other half, he's the kind
of boy

that will go out of his way every day for you,
whenever you want him to, whenever you asked

and i am just completely in awe of him,
i'm the tight chest of taking a test you didn't
remember to study for, i'm the sound of glass breaking,
i'm the kind of girl you fall asleep with
only to wake up alone,
i'm the kind of girl that breaks people like they are the
bindings on books

i leave messes where i have been. he cleans them up
without complaining. i press my worried palms against
his chest and try to shove in all of my broken past. he
keeps opening up to control it. i keep letting him down
and screwing him up and he keeps saying,
just being with you is reward enough.

"I met a man that makes my insides melt."

i am eighteen and cutting out squares of paper for my
newest d.i.y projects with the scissors i once
cut deep into myself with. i am trying to distract
myself from jumping in front of a train or maybe just
jumping on one with nothing but four dollars and a
peanut butter sandwich. her chest heaves when she
looks at me. "how are you so *perfect?"* she sighs,
flipping her blonde hair out of her eyes. i don't say
anything, just smile so tightly that it traps the scream
between my teeth. i pretend i am chewing and
swallowing her words until they are nothing but
feathers to me.

i am nineteen and i still wish i could return to the fifth
grade to fix every mistake i have made. my hands
shake whenever i put sugar in my coffee and
i have such bad anxiety that i can't go see a movie and
every second of every day i am shoving down the urge
to run away. she takes in my outfit and shakes her head
and says,
"how are you always dressed so excellently,"
and i want to explain that i just didn't sleep last night
because i suddenly became convinced that i was
forgetting something so i took apart my closet and
reorganized it because i get these compulsions to do
stupid things and unless i do them, terrible things will
happen to me or my loved ones. i shake my head and
do not tell her that i am obsessive. i don't mention that
i'm starting to think i need medication because i can't
leave the house without rapping on wood four eight
twelve times or locking and unlocking and locking the
door or folding and refolding this one particular shirt. i
pretend i am good at fashion instead of
bad at self-control.

i am twenty and she is drunk and i am tipsy and her
heels are city blocks taller than mine are. i am not
having fun because i don't actually like parties or
excessive drinking because i always fuck something up

on nights like these and then i lose friends because i'm a piece of shit and then i lose hope and then i spiral like a falling plane. in her beautiful dress she is leaning over a toilet while i hold back her hair and she's crying and begging me to change, she says, "i wanna be the perfect one for a change, why is it always you, why can't you just take a break." i don't say anything, just give her little bits of paper towel to wipe off her mouth because she has no idea the things i have done.
i wouldn't wish this *perfection* on anyone.

"She is everything I want to be."

the ten most common fears:

1. arachnophobia, fear of spiders, more common in females than in males; why at night she chokes on the idea of other fingers on you, long and thin.
2. ophidiophobia, fear of snakes; fear of being crushed alive by commitment, why in the mornings you never left your number waiting.
3. acrophobia, fear of heights; why you stayed away from people who could make you fall
in love, why looking at her
made you feel like throwing up.
4. agoraphobia, fear of situations where escape is difficult, fear of crowded areas and open spaces; fear of returning to a home that no longer feels comfortable, your fear of being in a room with girls like her.
5. cynophobia, fear of dogs; fear of the graves where good noses could dig up the mistakes you have made.
6. astraphobia, fear of thunder and lightning; of being terribly alone in a house which always sounds like both, the stormclouds of your history always behind closed doors.
7. trypanophobia, fear of injections; fear of ending up with her smile tearing through the heartstrings you've built up, fear of how she seems
to get straight to your blood.
8. social phobias, fear of social situations; your fear of how easy she makes this all seem, how quickly she can get a room laughing
9. pteromerhanophoba, fear of flying; fear of remembering the last time you felt alive because it will only lead to her, to what she can do
10. mysophobia, fear of germs or dirt; fear of kissing her because of how much it hurts.

"I drink to keep myself numb."

i am standing in the shower the first time i realize
that you no longer love me. it doesn't hit me like
bricks but instead like hot water, a slow wave that
starts at my toes and burns through my skin. i
do not cry. i tell myself i am making ghosts
where there is no haunting, that i am wrong -
but when i get out and start to dry off, i catch sight of
myself in the mirror. i drop eye contact. i look like i am
going towards my death with open arms.

we are sitting in a parked car and your hands clench
the wheel and i know you do not want me, but i say
"i love you, baby" anyway.
your eyebrows knit.
"can you not talk right now?" you ask, "i'm trying to
focus."

i want you to pull over. i want to kiss you hard
and trail nibbles down your jaw
with the same shaky passion
as the first time we made
contact. i want to remind you of that moment
because i can't stop thinking about it.

i am somewhere between being mad at myself
for giving you everything and being sad
because i still want to keep giving.
you open your palms and take what i offer
and i am left empty.
you fuck me in a bed that two weeks later will
smell of another girl.
i lean in to kiss you and you turn
away, just a little. i pretend not to notice.
i pretend
we are whole.
i take you in the shower with me
and get on

my knees.
i think of praying while
your hands tangle in my hair.

i think of how my mama raised me better
than to grovel for a boy's attention.
i think about how many times i ruined my own morals
for your satisfaction. i think about how many times
you've said,
"of course i love you honey," while we
were in bed, i think about long i have known
you are lying.

you are too caught up in sex to notice
i am crying.

"He says he loves me but I know he doesn't. Still, I don't want to lose him, so I pretend I believe him."

be around
for your best friend's eighteenth birthday
because else she's going to spend it alone,
slowly doing more shots than she should,
one for her and one for you since you always
promised you would do it with her.
i know because i am her.

be around for your little sister's high school years
or else she'll be so confused and alone and sad
that she'll start snorting cocaine in the bathrooms
and by the third year will have lost her willpower
to be somebody. i know this because i've seen it
happen.

be around for your own wedding, be around for your
thirtieth birthday party, be around to read the next
world-changing book, be around to write it, be around
to watch plays and to go to college and
fall asleep in libraries where strangers give you
blankets and to ride trains until you're no longer scared
of them and make art in pen on the back of your hands
when you're bored and to write poetry that sucks
until you can write poetry that doesn't and get so good
at violin that you accidentally end up becoming the
next big thing and to visit new york city and visit
disneyworld and to see the world

be around. there are so many things
you haven't yet found.

"I can't stop crying."

my brain is splatter-painting itself
like i'm modern art and you have to
watch me be a thunderstorm of low serotonin
and i feel sorry i'm making you sit
through this.

i am either shaking so badly i cannot focus
or i feel so tired i don't want to bother.
i am either sure i want to die
or terrified of the possibility. i am either
a short-fuse detonation or long-term
radiation, i am leaking, i am leaking,
i am falling apart in old copper pipes

and once a boy broke my heart and all i said
was, *it hurts less than i expected,* because
i was already so used to breaking myself

and once i almost felt happy but
don't worry it went away
before i could get attached to the feeling

and just for once just as a change
just as a new and exciting fun game

i'd like to feel like i'm
not insane.

"I have really bad depression and anxiety."

things about being the failure child:

1. honestly i think i'm pretty
fucked up, it's just that not
nobody really cares enough
to notice
2. i do not need to be reminded
about how much better everyone else is,
always scoring better on tests, always
doing more things.
whatever punishment you're going to give
isn't going to be cruel enough;
guaranteed,
late at night,
i'm going to torture myself worse than anything
you could ever dream up.
2. do you know that i would break apart
my very soul
just for you to be proud of me for even
one moment.
4. i know, i *know*:
at my age, my brother/father/uncle/our neighbor:
each managed to save the world and get jobs and
be special and useful and the best i can manage
is getting out of bed
5. when i make wishes, they all say the same
thing: that just once, you wouldn't look at me
like i'm your biggest disappointment.
6. there's so much pressure, all the time,
pouring out of your mouths and pushing into me
until i cannot breathe;
one of these days it's going to
explode from inside me
7. i'm so sorry i wasn't the kid you wanted
to raise. i'm
sorry,
just sorry,
okay.

"One day I want to be great, but I'm so scared I won't be."

family is not in the blood;
it is in the bones.

when your best friend knits her fingers with yours
so you feel less alone:
that is family.
when she puts your body between hers
and the screen during a scary movie
but would willingly fight anything real
that ever laid a finger on you, ever left the littlest
of wounds:
that is family.

family is when she eats
the last of your ice cream and
shouts just as loud as you do
when your favorite song comes on the radio.

family is not the fists of a father,
the sharp sullen brow of a brother.
it is not your duty to love people who only hurt you.

family is the sister
who waits until you're home to watch a show,
the mother who brings you flowers just because
you haven't told her you're feeling down
but somehow, she knows.

it's okay
to choose your family, to pick it
from where only kindness grows.

"I live in his shadow constantly."

doesn't it just fucking complicate things when
the inside of your body is a tattoo of black ash,
no regrowth in the package;
your outsides a messy cheap gin smile and
floral dresses and scars you never mention

nobody wants to learn that the girl
who acts like a housewife, like home, like happy
is actually two shots from
hospital drunk;
the girl has bruised her knees to go down on boys
who call her the wrong name, has fucked up
her metabolism, spoons up safe foods by the gallon
but won't touch potato chips because they've got too
many calories in them, wears scarves to cover hickies
and wears concealer for her dark circles,
constantly angry but dodges phone call because
they're too confrontational.

nobody cares if you're fucked up anymore.
they say *welcome to the real world, there's*
no one here
who will kiss those cuts.

it doesn't make me wanna grow up,
doesn't make me want to
somehow fight off this
fucking numb;

i just want to swallow nothing
but my own self
until there's
nothing
left.

"I feel empty, and I don't know what to fill myself with."

we are in the middle of our mac and cheese when
she announces that
girls with scars will never get husbands
and i choke. *it's awful for me to say,* she shrugs, *but
everyone knows they're attention whores.*

she's never seen my thighs due to an excessive amount
of effort and planning. i let no one close to me, even
girls like her that seem friendly.
i finally manage to cough enough that i can speak
before i can force the words
why do you think that? out of me.
she eats another spoonful and again raises
one slim shoulder blade, tossing her hair out of her
eyes to proclaim, *they just are. they're made
that way, i don't know.*

and she doesn't know. sometimes i feel hands grabbing
me, a slew of lies about who i am and what is
important to me, how i am filled with the sin of vanity,
that attention is a sin, that i am a whore
for wanting it:

if someone is taking a blade to their body in the hopes
anyone might notice, it's because they're drowning
and desperate for someone to pass them a rope, not
because they live on compliments alone.
sad people don't want to be coddled, held
until the blood stops, tourniquet children who
wrap tight around our friends until we suffocate them:
we know that when we
admit to things, we suddenly become
creatures of duct tape and dry prayer,
ugly. we don't want people to see this. we
don't want people to know.
who do you even think i wear long sleeves for?

"My best friend started cutting because she wanted attention."

when i was eleven,
you and i went out to the monkey bars and when i fell
my knee bled so badly you asked me,
why aren't you crying,
and i said, *it doesn't hurt bad enough.*

i think we made promises
to the insides of each other's palms
as if the lines there were perfect for signatures;
we were glass houses with each other
and knew every dark secret.
if someone started throwing rocks
we were all going to get blistered hands and feet.

in freshman year i broke my leg
and you held my hand in the ambulance and asked me,
why aren't you crying, and i said,
i'm saving those tears for a worse something.

you kissed her
under the umbrella
you accidentally
stole from me
two months ago.
she doesn't ever have
to call shotgun.
she knows where she's riding.
her lips are never chapped like mine.
she's always in one piece.

in sophomore year when
i got my heart broken clean in two
by some boy you swore to beat up
we watched action movies and you said,
i'm surprised you're not crying,
and i said, *he can't hurt me.*

it's been three fucking years. i still
watch you
hold the door open for her,

get her coffee. how you
light up when she talks to you.
i still listen to every stupid story
that comes spilling out of your mouth about
her.

on my birthday
for once it was
just you and me
and we got so drunk that
i forgot everything
and for a second
i had you close to me.

you got a call from her
and even though your body stayed with me,
i watched your heart leave.

you looked up and asked,
why are you crying?

"I'm absolutely in love with my best friend... is it bad I wish I was his girl?"

i.   when he says your name, it will come with a pause on both sides, as if the letters were padded with phrases he can't quite find the words to pronounce. his lips will form the word as if he's already practicing kissing you.

ii.   he will be in the middle of a sentence when you raise your eyes to his, and everything he was about to say will die on the mountains of his teeth. his heart will stop beating. maybe later when he reorients he will laugh about it, but know, in that moment, you made the rest of his world go quiet.

iii.   he will find ways to touch you without reason as if contact with your skin has become an addiction.

iv.   in the dead of night, he will still stand by you even as your soul goes dark. he will stand by you even into the early of dawn.

v.   you will be walking down an aisle at a truck stop, trying to locate the iced tea that you like even though they've been sold out of the watermelon flavor for the last four days and you send him a text to complain about it. he will ask you to come hang out to watch a dumb movie because who else would he invite
and when you show up at his door, a little shaky,
you will see the light come into his eyes.
both of you will stand there, just you and he,
and then he will ask you if you want the popcorn
buttered or salted or both
to go with your
watermelon iced tea.

"How do I know if a boy loves me?"

i think the stars got jealous
because i got to kiss you
and they only
got to watch

they must be laughing now;

i fell in love
       and you did not.

"He was so radiant."

we sit on the couch and he flips through our psych
homework and sighs and admits
that he doesn't quite believe in all the attention
depression gets,
that most people are just lazy and faking it, that they
could just do something to make themselves feel better
like
change their whole diet.

i want to say:
you cannot light a fire in space. we are only organic
compounds; we cannot make ourselves into energy
when there is none to be found.

i want to say:
the worst part isn't even the feeling sad, it's the feeling
happy for a moment because you're never sure if
you're better or this is just an illusion before things get
much worse. a cycle begins, the promise of happiness
only squashed by your own fear of it.
what if it doesn't stick. it's better to be numb than
have to lose it.

i want to say:
please give me the cure if you have it,
i want to be a success story about someone who
just changed their outlook and now feel
perfectly healthy.

but i know better than to be a burden.
i shrug and change the subject and
when i am bad again
i don't reach out
to text him.

"It might be the usual calm before the storm."

please tell me it gets easier,
that one day my hands won't shake,
my hips won't complain,
that i won't obsess about how much
i weigh

please tell me i learn to sleep easy,
that i get out of here, that i somehow
make money.

please tell me i haven't fucked up everything,
that i actually have a future instead of the
blankness
of the next four years
that i see coming

please tell me i find love
not in someone else's hands but
somewhere in my old heart, that i
am able to locate this locust selfhatred and
gnaw it out, that i learn to look in the mirror
and love who i see

because honestly
right now
i have no idea
who i am
or what i'm doing.

"I want to die more often than I want to live. Things are getting hard again."

you only ask to go out for the night,
but your mother still sighs
as if you're seventeen stones balanced on her lungs.
when she says *you're never home anymore,*
you feel so guilty that you cancel plans.
later you will go numb,
scrolling your facebook feed
that features pictures you never got to be in.
your friends will talk about that night
for four more weeks.

you tell your friend that you can't make it
to her party because it's your father's birthday but
she looks so hurt that
you end up going;
only to spend the whole night staring at a wall
while everyone else gets stupidly drunk,
holding back her hair because she drinks too much,
babysitting them all instead of having fun.
when you get home
your family won't even look at you,
talking around you as if they are a river and you are
alone.

you tell your teachers
that you're having difficulty
getting homework done. half don't care and
the rest just give you extra. you stay up into the nights
where the bad things live, where your brain becomes
rot on a stem,
chased by thoughts that
devour your joy. you get high grades
but you're so tired you're dizzy.
at home,
you're just doing what's expected.
at school,
you're an annoying little teacher's pet.

you take a break from friends for homework and they
hate you

so you take a break from family for friends
and then your family hates you and finally
you quit everything
because you're about to explode
and the pressure you're under
has a riptide hold.
you're worthless, now, no friends,
no real home.
you can't even get your
schoolwork done.

you are playing a game you have never
actually
won.

"The only way I know to be happy is if I choose to disappoint everyone else."

we had a sword fight with mozzarella sticks
and then argued about who deserved the last piece
even though we both knew it was me;
later we'd both describe our perfect partners,
trying desperately to pretend we weren't
just describing each other.

we jumped under the covers
to watch bad movies and
"just friend cuddle,"
told ourselves
we were only close to keep warm,
ended up
falling
asleep in each other's arms.

when we woke up, i don't mention
that i dreamed of you.

when our friends ask us
about the other person, we answer:
there's nothing going on, we're just
friends, nothing new

and both of us
wish
it wasn't
true.

"I think I'm falling for my best friend."

a letter of apology to the boy nobody ever stuck with:

when we were in first grade we got married and i asked
if we had to kiss. when you said *yes*, i panicked and
shoved you to the ground as hard as i could. we were
best friends again in an instant but i must have taught
everybody else something, didn't i, because even
though i never purposefully hurt you ever again,
it wasn't the last time you were pushed down,
was it?

in eight grade we were in two different friend groups
and you didn't know i was getting bad and starting to
lust after the pain of paper cuts;
if i had known you were thirteen and already set to ruin
yourself, i would have run to your house in my bare
feet and begged you to stay with me
but at that time i barely remembered
i had promised to love you if
you loved me

in freshman year we reconnected and i realized
somehow i was falling in love again;
you made me laugh so hard i couldn't breathe
and let me cry over dumb romance movies.
the two of us were just gawky awkward stupid teens;
i was selfish, thought the broken one was
me

i am twenty years old and still tell your story.
your mother calls on the anniversary.

i wish i could have done something.

"I'm so sorry I let you down."

a year ago
my thighs were shredded with thin lines.
i never felt alive anymore,
just as if i was
sitting around,
waiting to die.

i still have bad days,
count calories absentmindedly,
almost accidentally,
still keep a blade with me,
have numb months,
dark weeks, endless nights
filled with the agony
of being
nothing

but i am alive.

i didn't expect to be.

so many beautiful things have happened to me.
i ran into the woods and the woods grew into me,
we all went skinny dipping, i taught campfire songs
to people in the street, dyed my hair,
learned how to say *i love you,* took up dancing,

and maybe i'm not completely alright,
but for once
i actually want to keep this life

so just keep going,
getting better,
having adventures, okay?
you and i deserve
another
beautiful
day.

"I honestly don't plan on living..."

hey babe, maybe you forgot
but last night you swore you'd call in the morning;
i suppose promises you make while crawling
between my knees
aren't exactly holy so

i'm trying not to care
about how much you ignore me
or how you leave as soon as we're finished
like you're burning, or how
you don't really think to see if i'm happy.

i keep writing poetry in the shape of you
fucking me.
our bodies connecting like we were
trying to bury our bones in the bedframe,
blood on our lips and bruises like necklaces.
in the pulpit of my ribs
you whisper a prayer:
of course i love you, darling.

but you
don't
and you
never
did.

"We spent the summer fucking nearly every night. You would never call me yours, though."

my mama says the first time she knew
i was too kind for my own good,
an alley cat came into our lawn and i spent
the better part of six hours trying to coax it
into eating. i still have scars on my hand
from getting too close too quickly.
i got mad at myself for scaring him, instead
of crying.

mama must have been wrong, though,
because whenever people give me their hearts
i always find some way to gently return them,
unused, unopened, hardly even unwrapped.
i am better with dogs than i am with people,
better at trusting them, better at staying close.
people need you to explain why you love them,
what you're doing; people are complicated
and messy while i bet no dog ever told her master,
*i just feel like you don't give as much in this
relationship as i do.*

i'm bad at loving loudly. i'm the kind who leaves
little notes and wears your sweaters around and
writes you poems,
not the kind that shows up with a boombox.

i wish people were more like animals,
could come and go out of your life without
messy bits in between

just pure love.
simple and clean.

"It kills you to hurt them."

i honestly
don't even
know
what
exactly
is wrong with me
anymore.

"I keep pushing her away. I don't even know why."

i start mornings looking into the mirror
staring at my crooked broken
witch nose,
aim a curse at my own eyes:
"he doesn't love you, so don't try."

the mirror just
glares right back, follows my path
into the shower. i look down
to my toes, over the slow hill
of a curved stomach. i do not cry here,
just rub soap over all the parts that hurt
and sing to myself, "he doesn't love you,
he doesn't love you, you're the worst."

and then i'd see you and suddenly
everything gets a good kind of
quiet
in my head

you make me laugh harder than i thought
was possible, make me feel safe in places i panic,
find adventure with me in the simplest of activities
and you make my life so incredibly happy
that i go to bed with
a dumb smile on my lips,
wondering when i get to see you again

only to wake up after nightmares,
all soaked in sweat,
in the darkness alone,
having to whisper, "he won't
ever
love you,
he just
won't."

i made the mistake of believing that
your bones were a good place
to grow roots and now i miss you
because people aren't gardens but

my great-grandmother used to say
that ghosts don't haunt houses,
ghosts haunt people;
if you feel empty and cold it's because
your soul is out there
wandering the streets with the person
you call home

so even though i'm alone
and frozen, a plant with no water, a sun
without heat

i'd like to think
you're still somehow
with me.

"I want to go home to the people I love."

in the middle of the crowd, panic rises up my throat
but she looks over one shoulder, smiles wide,
grabs my hand and straightens her spine,
promises me, *if anyone touches you, i'll fight them off;*
hell, give me a reason, i'll fight
everyone

she has always been my sentinel,
angel with a flaming sword,
guiding light in every storm.
she is the child
of wind and fire,
somehow, impossibly,
every bad thing that happens to her
just makes her grow brighter.

i want to kiss her whenever she's talking,
or distracted, or singing, or asleep,
kiss her in every instant but
i am a steamship full of demons.

one night i am too drunk to hold myself back,
the two of us lying on her floor,
laughing about something stupid, and
in the comfortable silence of the night, i find
my mouth blurting
i am festering with bad thoughts,
flinching before i'm even done.
she grabs my hand like she is saving me
from drowning,
holds tight while i begin to sob, her eyes
locked on mine while she whispers,
i know, and i am trying to fight every one of
those thoughts
off.

"I am in love with my best friend, but she doesn't know how fucked up I am."

---

i've tried to be honest
about the catastrophe in my head
but the minute i sit down
to write something

i only end up with
the same sad idea on repeat:

i'm sad pretty
constantly.
i don't know why
but i want
to stop
breathing.

the funny thing is
i'm really not doing well,
but i happen to be excellent
at making people see heaven
when i'm going through hell

i mean you can fill pages
and pages
with verse -
none of it matters because
if you are empty,
so are your word

i'm serious, i probably need help,
but then again, how would you
know

there's more darkness in me than
any poetry
shows.

"I don't know what to write about."

sometimes i think i do this all on purpose,
that i pour sadness down my throat
because i'm so familiar with the smooth caress
of rock bottom
that being anywhere else feels unsafe,
unnatural, unstable:
it's happiness i cannot handle.

i never could write
when i was doing okay.

effortless, i sabotage myself;
only to get mad at those who are
doing well.
like i'm stuck in one place and
everyone should be suffering with me,
while at the same time,
i would wish this
on nobody.

i just could have been more,
you know?

i'm the only reason i haven't yet made it
to shore. i'm who destructs all my hope.
who slices until there's nothing left. who
drowns in the sea.

i am what is destroying me.

"I fear I will never start to pursue my dreams."

WHY I CAN'T:
- the idea of my mother crying makes my chest hurt
  worse than when i get asthma attacks
  except there's no inhaler for when your
  heart collapses
- my sister is still so young she'll always
  be my little girl,
  and i need to protect her
- today i had like four brownies in a very scientific test
  to see if deliciousness wore off,
  and it did not
- clean laundry still feels amazing
- my room is messy and should not be given as a burden
  to anybody
- being behind in a class is not a permanent problem nor
  are grades honesty that important
- i want to go exploring
- there are many plants i haven't yet seen
- listening to AC/DC still makes me feel like
  i'm a wild animal hunting down weaklings
- even on the worst days,
  at the very least,
  my bed is amazing
- and so is sleep
- if you're dead you cannot dream
- for love of
  everyone else
- one day that love
  will be for
  myself.

my brother sees me
at sixteen,
lying drunk on the floor and crying,
and when i ask him
how i get rid of someone, he
grabs a pen
and starts writing his
"mathematically proven" list
for forgetting it:

1. change your ringtone for every person,
   silence notifications.
2. cut your hair or wear it up or dye it dark.
3. find a friend to do things with you
   so that your free time doesn't
   ache for the loss of him,
   so that your brain relearns to be able
   to just do things without him
   again.
4. change is imperative,
   stagnation means death,
   remind yourself that growth
   is how we escape emptiness.
5. replace him,
   but not with a new man.
   find a new hobby, a new book series,
   a new poet, a new playlist.
   fill up your time with things
   100% not tainted
   by him.

my brother tacks it to my wall,
explains that we miss people
because
our brains
like bad habits,
that after
21 days of not thinking
about it,
you don't even notice

that you have forgotten about it.

he draws an equation under his list:
includes all of his ingredients:

$$healing = \frac{(\text{sum of above}) + (\text{self love})}{(\text{time} + \text{patience})}$$

he says the catalyst to all of this
is just believing
that one day
i can be
over it.

"How do you deal with breakups?"

you don't get it,
okay.

i know people always say
"everyone gets anxiety"
but not like
this

not like skipped classes,
convinced death is coming,
three-degree weather and sweating
from it, almost shaking out of my skin,
throwing up in public buildings,
endlessly counting exits,
coming up with escape strategies,
not like terror, not like
slipping out from control,
not like
don't even feel in my body
anymore.

it is not the nervous of a public speech, it is
debilitating,
irrational and
all-consuming.

"I hate having anxiety."

i try to explain
that i'm insecure,
feeling the words come out like
an apology, awkward and gawky, a fish out of water,
flopping around in the shape of letters
as i try to make:

"i need affirmation every minute of the day
and to hear that you still like me, i need to hear you
don't think i'm ugly, that you didn't randomly fall out
of love with me, that you don't still think about her
every evening, that you'd rather think of me,
i need to hear a whole lot of things"

somehow sound like i'm not
fucking crazy.

it gets tangled in the air and i end up blurting,
you never got rid of her perfume instead.

you shrug a little, eyes on your phone,
facebook feed, *never got around to it*, you tell me.
don't even look up from what you're doing.

i want to say to delete her, that i don't understand
how you live in a world where she is all around you,
that you carry her with you, sleep with her
filling up your room

but i just go silent.

it's too loud in my head.

"My boyfriend keeps things that his exes left in his room and it makes me insanely jealous."

i'm trapped between wanting someone to notice
and wanting to be left alone

i mean my doctor pointed out my scars and
some part of me wanted to speak up,
to spill over the examination table like a tidal wave,
come crashing down in a puddle at her feet,
explain the white hot high i need,
some part of me wanted to beg for help
because when my skin heals
i don't even recognize myself

but instead before i knew what i was doing
i had told her that the cat left perfectly parallel
claw marks on my body and since
i laughed and talked about how he didn't
mean to make me bleed,
she completely bought my story.

i'm too good at lying.
even the people who know what i'm doing
don't know how bad i can be
because i'm too good at making jokes
like i'm not struggling. i pull magic tricks,
wave my hands, create illusions,
make it sound like a phase, like
stopping would be easy.

there is no unharmed part of my body.
i've been doing this since thirteen
and in two months
i turn twenty-three.

nobody ever came to save me.

"Even my best friend and boyfriend think I've stopped cutting and I've lied to them all, but I can't stop."

everyone makes love sound like
rocks against the window at two in
the morning, like grand gestures in
front of the classroom, like public displays
of affection and eighty-two rose bouquets
and maybe that is a part of it but

when real love hits you, he will be
spreading hummus across flatbread, sleep
tangling fingers in his hair, a slight
wispy smile on his lips like he knows
the world's greatest secret and even though
you're both standing in the kitchen's
bad lighting and you're both still
recovering from napping and you're
only in your socks and undies,
it will feel like you're standing next to a jet plane
during takeoff, it will just knock you right over

when real love hits you, she will be sitting
in front of a bad action movie, eyes on
the screen and legs tangled between yours,
her body fitting so perfectly against you that you
feel like the two of you are puzzle pieces made for
each other, the warmth of her laughter
like whiskey through your veins
and you will realize you have spent the
last five minutes just looking
at her face and maybe the two of you
illegally downloaded this film and maybe her
fingertips are covered with popcorn butter and
maybe you'll never be able to form a good enough
way to tell her, but just even seeing her happy makes
your heart explode like a snowball against
a windowpane, you're just completely wrecked by it

when love hits you,
they will be absently licking icing
off the back of their knuckle while they make cupcakes
for their whole class and their nose will wrinkle and
you will find an inexplicable humor in how
they literally sprint from the room in order to
sneeze without breathing on the food, you will watch
the way they sneak some batter from the bowl with a
hooked finger, how their left cheek has a little smear of
flour right across
where their freckles rest like clovers and maybe they
are not the best baker in the world but
even if they burn everything they make you,
you realize you wouldn't care, you would
honestly eat whatever it was for
rest of your life because it means being
close to them and that idea just cracks
against your ribs like how rain always sings as
it falls, so in love with the ground that it
praises the earth as it hits

and this is what love is:
the moments of looking up and finding
you're with the world's most perfect person,
so full of flaws and such a terrible, terrific
fit.

"This is silly, but he's home to me."

some people don't remove easily.
they don't slip out from
under your skin without
a lot of scrubbing.
some of them are tattoo machines,
burn into us in what feels like
a permanent way.

his fingerprints are seared into my skin.
i still don't feel clean when i think of him.
maybe the bones he broke healed long ago
but i flinch whenever someone
raises their voice
and while i am technically whole,
i can still feel a
split down my soul.

the worst part is,
unless you're covered with blood,
everyone thinks you're just fine enough.
they do anything to
dismiss your pain.

last night i thought i heard him laughing
and froze to my seat.
four days ago someone was wearing his cologne
and i almost threw up in the hallway.
it doesn't always wash out. he's still in your hair,
but people get tired of hearing about it. he's still
under your sheets,
but people get used to the fact that you don't sleep.
it doesn't wash out

but you do get better at living dirty.

my mother says time heals all wounds;
it's more that they fade.
that you get better
at being wounded
every day.

that you become better
at treating yourself
the way you deserve.
somewhere in all the hell,
you teach yourself to heal, to
undo the damage he dealt.

time helps, but it is you,
relearning to love yourself.

i want to believe
that eventually,
your skin heals, your soul mends,
it all goes away
and the good news is
that i know already:

you get stronger.
it gets easier to be
okay.

HOW TO GET OVER A BOY
in six simple steps:

i. remind yourself of every time he kissed you
when you were too sad for it. think of how
you tried to explain the hollowness you could hear
inside of your limbs but he just asked if that meant
no more sex. remind yourself of every time you
went dark for no reason
but he still couldn't tell
you were suffering.
remind yourself of the times you
swallowed down your darkness
just because you didn't want to bother him.

ii. write your name out with his last name attached.
realize you would have given up who you are
for him. realize it takes you away from yourself.
realize your initials
wouldn't look right anymore.
realize that in the end,
you kept who you are.
realize you didn't give him
everything.
you don't have to start over from nothing.
write out your relationship in red pen.
circle the problems. highlight them. write bad poetry
and call your blog something dramatic and enigmatic
like "red blood, black ink,"
maybe you'll find out that what you have to say
people want to read
maybe you'll find better support
for your art than he ever gave maybe you'll find
that creation makes you happy in some small way.
write him out of your veins.

iii. cry, drink whiskey, cry,
eat ice cream. i know your insides
feel ugly, but trust me, dress nicely.
wear thigh highs out to get
coffee, wink at truck drivers, get nasty.
paint your lips red.
wear your hair out of your face. feel beautiful for
four minutes.
at the five-minute mark,
you can go back home
and lay down until your heart stops hurting.
don't cry,
you've got good makeup on.
drink milk even if it's almond milk,
your liver and bones are
going to thank you.
call your mom.
go shopping. pick out a whole new wardrobe
he's never seen.
get something in every color. go somewhere cheap
where they have lacy bras for like a dollar.
buy eight, buy sixteen. drink
vodka. go out and party.
show off your G-string. feel
wanted
again.

iv. keep your eyes closed when you are trying to sleep.
do not reach for him. get a dog or a cat or a lizard if
you can't be alone.
find out that animals love with less conditions
and more honesty.
count stars. count cars. count raindrops.
replay bioshock, go out and buy it if you don't
already own it. replay portal,

it's phenomenal and you know it.
replay the things you both said, realize you
aren't the only one to blame for all of this.
replay his last good voicemail and then erase it.
take a deep breath and select every text.
delete all of them. do not read them first, you will
feel each word like knives.
if you do make the mistake
of reliving what he said, try reading it aloud in a
mocking tone. i find childish mimicry is often quite
soothing. when he posts things on facebook, close your
eyes, close the tab,
close the laptop.
go for a walk even though it's too cold.
maybe get a second cat. there's always room
for a second cat.

v. whenever you are sad, wash your hands. my mother
says being clean is the most powerful pick-me-up
in the whole
universe.
go shower until your fingertips
wrinkle up.
get new sheets
with a higher thread count than you really need.
renovate your apartment, it will make you feel like
your insides are shifting around too.
renovate you. cut off your hair, dye it, get a tattoo,
pierce your ears or septum
or where the sun don't shine.
go punk rock for however long
you want to be punk rock,
realize you're not quite confrontational enough
for a mosh pit but you like their music,
go indie, go k-pop, go crazy. why the fuck not.

whenever you are sad,
find ten new songs.
whenever you are sad,
text a friend and ask how they're doing.
whenever you see a couple in public,
do not think of him. think of mopping. wash your
insides. be clean, but totally have sex
in a public restroom. whenever you are sad,
paint your nails and then take a shower.
watch the color flake off, sigh, repaint them.
change your outfit.
whenever you are sad, call your mother or
your sister or someone else you love.
if you have no one, call my mother,
she's super nice but she'll totally make you clean the
house until you feel better – although, to
be honest, it will
actually
make you feel better.

vi. breathe. breathe. breathe.
you'll get there eventually.

"How to get over him."

watching you drift from me was
knowing the sun and still having
to live in winter

we were continents that collide once
and then drift off from each other forever.
i'm still left with the mountain ranges
you pushed into me, long jagged canyons
where i met your lips, your teeth. i am
a land mass with an ocean in my lungs,
saltwater memories

i move my hands in cloudbanks over
the drumlins of my hipbones
and think of your glacier fingertips
that left little rivulets of blood wherever
you held on, trenches in my skin
that once felt like passion but might have
just been desperation.

i am a caldera of a girl, all hollow inside
where used to be heat
and you,
you're still volcanoes, still burning

it's just new nations you're warming the beds of,
new girls with new forest eyes and new secrets
and the clear of their open-sky hearts.

i am the storm,
underwater,
left alone in the dark.

"It seems as if he doesn't care at all. I just want to move on."

the truth is
nothing serious is really happening
in my life,
no real reason
to feel like the walls
are crumbling in on all sides

the truth is
if i could just
get my shit together
i'd be fine

the truth is
i don't think i could save myself
even if i
tried.

she said,
"get to know him and
you'll love him."

it was the single greatest mistake
she would ever make
because he and i started to become best friends
and my heart
started pounding against my ribs and
i knew it was wrong and i hated myself
for it

when the night got silent and her steady breathing
filled the air between us, he whispered over
her sleeping form,
"i fucked up"

we both know our skin will never touch
because my love for her
is stronger than my love of myself
and i will never hurt her as
long as i can help it

every time his smile makes me warm
and he makes me laugh, i feel the world
go black. he's the first person to call
on my birthday
and i feel a pull to him like gravity,
sun and earth

if we touch
one will burn

dear lord
forgive me
i dream to
betray
her.

"I'm in love with my friend's boyfriend."

anything i can do, you can do better.

i mean
your waist is the size of one of my thighs
even though i've been eating healthy since
i was eleven and
your grades are always higher even if
only by a few points but
for some reason i feel every number
like a dagger and
you always have really amazing friends
because people flock to you
without thinking
and when you walk into a room
people stare at you like they're
trying to figure out if they're
in a dream and
the worst part is
you make it all look so
goddamn
easy

every time i think my feet
are solid beneath me, that i've found something
that's just for me, a talent,
a new hobby
you try it out for laughs
only to discover again that
you were just born better
in all aspects.

i'm no longer surprised
when you're naturally gifted
in the things i have to
struggle for.

i just don't want to care anymore.

"Everything I want to be is trapped inside her and I can't stand it."

i guess i'm kind of an unfair person,
say that something is "no big deal"
when i really mean,
"if you're not there it will
crush me"

i know logically
you're not a mind-reader
and i should stop
testing people to see
if they know me better
than to just let stuff go

i guess i just wish
that when i say
"i'm fine,"
someone would say,

"are you sure?"

"I didn't hear from him, even on Christmas."

just because he smiled at you
in the hallway today
doesn't mean anything.
he's a nice person, don't
make it into something it's not.
he probably didn't even
mean it for you. maybe he
had a nice thought.

so what if he says hello, so what
if he asks about your day and if
your math class got better.
he probably just thinks it's hilarious
that you stutter and blush.
maybe he's just cordial.
he'll never choose you to be his partner
for the new project so stop picturing it.

maybe he's started to sometimes hang out with you,
but it's probably some long-term joke.
don't think about how he finds
little ways to touch you,
he's just affectionate.
it means nothing.

it doesn't matter what you see,
you're lying to yourself to be happy.
nothing you do will be good enough

so just give up.

"He isn't in love with me."

the only thing
at which
i actually excel

is slowly and completely

destroying myself.

and i could fit a fist in the gap between my thighs
but i couldn't feel beautiful so i assumed maybe
i was doing skinny wrong,
more collarbones more coffee
less control over what was killing me

thank god for every food that broke my fast
even though i cursed its poor existence and
tried to puke it, thank god for every crumb and
calorie that kept me living

thank god for recovery, for hair that shines
like the setting sun, for fingernails that don't
flake off, for hipbones that don't bruise just by
looking at them, for hands that are strong enough
to hold onto the ones i love instead of
shaking so hard that they cannot write
a poem, thank god for the people who saw me at
my worst, for the boy who stood next to me
when my knees hit the ground
and i sobbed for an hour,
thank god for the girl who kept sending me text
messages about how good being healthy is
until i finally believed them, thank god for
the love spilling out like liquor over these bones
until i finally got better, so yes
my tummy is round now like

a smooth hill and my thighs kiss each other
like a desperate couple and my arms are puffed up
with pride

and i fucking love it
because i am alive.

"I find being able to cross my legs an accomplishment."

before i met you i had already burned out
so when you stuck your fingers into my ashes
and told me there was some hint
of leftover warmth,
that i might still
be a hearth
i almost fainted

i mean i've been living off of coffee
and been watching my dreams and aspirations
get soggy
i've been so shaky that
even i'm confused how i'm
still standing

you make me feel safe
like an oversized sweater,
you make me smile when i didn't think
things could get better,
you make me happy
with so little effort yet

you're my whole series of books
but in your story
i'm just a chapter.

"He makes me feel whole again, but he doesn't love me."

just because sad girls can smile

and broken boys won't let you see them cry

just because people who hurt might look happy

doesn't mean they don't want to die.

"She looked at me and said, "I thought you were stressed? It doesn't seem like it. I guess that, like your depression last year, was just in your head."

i just sometimes feel
like there is something evil
in these veins of mine
and maybe that all sounds
overdramatic
but i swear i don't know
my own mind

i feel like i'm not
always
in control;
after the horizon swallows the sun, and
the darkness spreads over my floor
into my bones,
suddenly the only thing i know
is the hush-quiet suggestions
of voices that want
terrible noise

and i just have to sit there
willing myself into sleep,
into staying on this earth,
being calm, being
whole, into
being less
of a burden

i don't want to be
this kind of person.

"I'm not crazy."

the first time i admitted it to myself it
was five days after and the clouds were so heavy
that i pictured god smoking a giant cigar,
just lying back and puffing out these
big fat grey bodies, his feet propped up, his mouth
sighing "fuck" on the exhale. i pictured god beside me
while we stood at your tombstone, just him and me and
my little body. i had all this space to fill up, this huge
gaping hole where you had been, a crack in my life
that i needed words or expensive dijon mustard
or copious amounts of alcohol to fill. i knew i was
expected to say goodbye but it didn't really feel like
your body was under my feet,
more like this was some kind of a joke and i was going
to see the hidden cameras at any moment.

"my best friend is dead," i said, just to test the way it
sounded. it hung in the air like mist.
i wanted to pop the letters like soap bubbles
but instead i just pat-patted your tombstone and walked
away.

two years after this i am very drunk
and we are playing a round of truth or dare with a
bunch of seniors. i like the one with eyes so blue they
are electric and he and i are swapping looks and
pressed up against each other and
we've already played that card game which is just an
excuse to kiss. i can't remember if we've made contact
on purpose.

"okay, okay, okay," says somebody, "person with the
saddest truth wins this round," he says, "gotta be true."

and we go around and i count: just broke up, car got
stolen, dog has cancer.
they get to me, electric blue stares into my eyes and the
music pumps and we're all full up

with the idea of getting some
and i hear myself say it for the second time in my life,
"my best friend died," and it doesn't shake when it hits
the air and everyone else goes silent. "he committed
suicide," i say.

"this round sucks," someone shouts, "everybody
drinks, let's do another."

we drink. blue kisses me. later he takes me to his bed
and asks if it's true, i say it is, he asks what happened, i
shrug, say, "don't want to talk about it," go down on
him before he has a chance to think about it.

last night i ate eighty-four peanuts because i like how
salty they are against my tongue. last night i looked in
the mirror and parted my hair to the right and then the
left and then down the center. last night i put on red
lipstick. last night i put on a black dress. last night i
took a moment to let down the walls and be myself. the
boy i like didn't text me back. the girl i like has no idea
and i'm gonna keep it like that. the memories i've
made are all so quiet against the silence in my head.

last night i was putting on my shoes and just stood
there for a second and for no reason at all,
heard myself say, "my best friend is dead."

i still haven't cried about it.

"*I love him. I love him. But he's dead*"

they say shit like
"oh just go out and buy a plane ticket to
anywhere, go live life instead of worrying about him"
but who actually has the time or the cash for that
so instead i've opened the college-girl manual on
how to scrub a boy out
from every strand of hair
he ran his fingers through,
instead i've started figuring out
the little things to make him wash out like
dip-dying your hair with the leftover bleach
from your sister's kit
or maybe using red kool-aid for it
so when you stand in the shower you watch
thin blood-colored streams
run down your curves
or maybe you learn to give your phone to
a more responsible adult when you go out to get drunk
because you kind of turn into a needy little shit
(you're starting to worry your friends are totally done
with it) and you start learning how to force yourself
into having fun in little thing
like spooning chocolate icing out of the container even
though it's probably definitely not healthy
but it's better than going crazy trying
to get thin again for him,
you learn not to let yourself get too introverted on
rainy days because
that shit is a slippery slope
right down into spending four hours
on his facebook page,
you learn to take long walks when you need to think
because that way at least you get some exercise since
let's be real
you really just want to curl up in bed and stare at a wall

until
the earth crumbles around your ears, you learn to dress
hot as hell just for yourself
because you're bammin-slammin-bootylicious,
you learn to be cool with leggings as pants
despite the fact
when you were fourteen and trying too hard
to be 'alternative' you totally used to rage
about how they're not actually,
you learn and you grow up
and you cry about it some and then you
cry about it until it feels like
you're gonna drown and then you have a couple of
days of just
absolute blankness
where you
kind of don't know if you're okay and then you have a
couple of days of being like hell yeah and then maybe
you see two people kissing and you start crying all
over again and it's okay
because you learn to stretch out in the sun
and to pet every animal you come across even if it's
something you're kind of scared of
and you learn and you learn and you learn and you
kind of end up
becoming a whole different person

and this will fuck with your head for a little
because whenever you see him
part of you will want to tell him
"i'm someone completely
new now,
i've buffed out some of my
flaws and i'm pretty fucking proud"

but at the same time you
don't want to go back to where you were
so you're in this weird
"do i actually talk to him"
limbo

you learn that you still feel an odd kind
of queasy when you think about him and you really
wanna puke when you see him with her
but you learn to take a deep breath
and not let it ruin your night and
to make out with random guys
if you're into that and
you learn to do your homework on time and you
learn the people you can study with so you can copy
from them and you relearn how to make friends
and you learn that you're not the only one
feeling broken and
you learn to be fine without him

because eventually
some part of you remembers that you've had a whole
life without him
and you were doing pretty good beforehand and
right now you might cry all day
but you're getting better and
you're gonna be
okay.

"I'm alone again and I'm not so sure I'm ever going to be loved."

i have about fourteen pairs of green socks
six green shirts
four green sweaters
and not that you asked but yes
two bras (one mint, one dark)
and i try to pretend it's because i love green
but more likely it's because
one time you said it was your favorite color

and this is a dumb thing to cry about
but i'm standing in a towel
staring into a laundry basket
and i can only find green socks

and i can only think about how when the sun shines
through your eyes they turn amber
or how when you smile at me i feel like
you have tipped liquor into my system
or how i don't even know if i like green more
than any of the other colors
but i still fucking went out and bought -
what is this, like, fifty? seventy? i don't know
but it's high –
green goddamn socks

i'm so fucking pathetic because i'm literally
desperate enough for your attention
that i'd strip naked
if you just asked for it

but today she wore red
the color of sunsets and passion

and you leaned over and whispered to me
doesn't she look good in that?
i think she knows it's my favorite
color.

"*I see them together every day and it crushes me inside.*"

you broke me so perfectly that it was almost natural to you. i remember standing there staring at my hands and wishing i could grip the top of my head and just tear down the center. you made me feel like paper. you made me feel like i had swallowed the night and it had sloshed like ink all over my insides.

i just don't know what i did to you to make it so easy for you to hate me

whatever it was, trust me,

i'm sorry.

"I didn't know words could hurt that much."

they will tell you that adulthood smells of
cities, of overcooked ramen noodles,
of four white cubicle walls
that close endlessly inward, of being lucky to have a
job even in a hostile environment, of refusing to
complain despite burdens you can't carry, of watching
your innocence fall out with your hair, of love that is
dispassionate, of settling down just to make your
parents happy, of your best friend's marriage going
catastrophic by month eight, of having children you
only half-want and who ruin your life for it

but

it instead smells of chocolate chip pancakes whenever
you want them, of putting brownie mix in the waffle
iron just to see if it works, of paperwork, but also of
wedding cake

it's not going to be easy. you can make it fun anyway.
you'll get tired, you'll get sad. you'll get
beat down by your boss and by coming home with
headaches and a sob in your throat.

but growing older doesn't always mean growing up.
you can still test your skills on the monkey bars, can
still go to see the princesses at amusement parks.

you can still find adventure. happiness. innocence. joy.
it's okay to get older. it's okay.

you've just got to take things day by day.

"Growing up and dying are actually synonyms."

she said i look ugly with my hair pulled back, that
maybe i should hide behind it because
nobody wants to see
the round moon of my face, not all of it, anyway
and later the boy i loved would tell me
he finds me pretty annoying and was wondering
if i wouldn't mind losing a few pounds
and after class my science teacher told me
to stop trying so hard, that i was a painful disaster to
watch, that i should just allow failure into my heart

and i don't care.

i am rivers and streams and their hatred cannot stop
me. i will find the ocean again, i swear it. one day i am
going to claw my way out of this shithole town and i
will bite down on life and leave my teethmarks in
everything i come across,
i'm going to have full novels to tell my kids,
going to be a storybook
on survival
just you wait

i'm going to get out of this.

"I can't wait to get an apartment with my best friend and live a simple life."

robert frost wrote about two roads in the woods
and i'm sitting in english class and i'm thinking
"what an asshole"
because two roads diverge
right between you and i
and his poem is more about discovering the wild in life
but for some reason i'm still
fucking crying

because you and i are like tree trunks
torn apart by lightning, we grew so close
for so long and
now we have to learn how to live without the other
person there with us
and i know it's just high school but i really fucking
love you

and i don't want to look back in ten years and realize
that i have no idea if you're even alive,
i don't want our only correspondence to be
the occasional retweet and half-hearted
facebook-reminded birthday wish,
i don't want to look back on this
and realize i lost something perfect

two roads diverge in these woods of our futures
and i can't follow where you walk.
you are going alone and
i'm left behind to be
the friend you forgot.

"I'm going to miss him very much. I don't know if I'll see him much now that he's graduating."

everybody sees this huge smile and endless kindness
and they think it's just because
i was born nice
but actually it's because
i know what it's like to hurt so badly inside
that you feel nothing at all
and i would wish this on no one.

everyone sees this hardworking girl
that is always willing to let you copy her homework
but they don't see the hours of anxiety,
of worrying about every possible thing i could have
forgotten, of the strange panic that comes at the idea
of just saying no to anything

everybody sees someone put together
instead of someone falling apart
everyone sees someone
competent
talented
whole

someone
i am not.

---

*"Everyone sees this perfect girl... I look in the mirror and I see someone else
entirely."*

you taught me to like my coffee black
because it was bitter like being with you

one of the worst feelings in this world
was hearing you list all the things that
make you hate someone
and sitting there realizing that you were
listing character traits i have like
straight-across bangs and a weird laugh
and wear converse with dresses
so i switched to boots that don't fit
and hair in a different style and
don't laugh much anymore.
you said you hate anyone who talks too loud
and overly insecure girls so
i speak quiet now, put my hand over my mouth
to muffle the sound
and never mentioned how the voices are
so fucking loud

i want you out of my life and i really regret
that i let myself change so that i could
please you.

i'm stuck with the scars you left on me
no matter what i do.

"My group of close friends have turned on me. It hurts but what hurts more is that I don't miss them."

you just mess with my head
like i'm your favorite
experiment

i swear i don't get it
sometimes you act like i am your favorite music,
like you would distill me
into wine bottles and sip me in a bubble bath
and sometimes
i'm radioactive, somebody you can't give
the time of day,
somebody who will
melt up your insides with my poison
and then
two days later you act like
nothing bad ever happened

i just don't get you. i don't know what
you're trying to do to me.
one minute i'm your best friend
and the next,
i'm your enemy.

i'd just like some sign from you
that this isn't some slow torture game
you're playing

and if it is,
please stop.
i promise
you're winning.

"He told me I was the perfect friend, and then he didn't talk to me for two weeks."

she was six and so was i and we sat under a tree that
had leaves shaped like little hearts and we promised we
would be best friends forever and her eyes were the
color of the sky when it's so blue it's almost hard to
look at and she had the kind of laugh that made
everyone around her start to chuckle.

she was eight and so was i and we were in dance class
with our feet turned out and our heads held high and
our teacher came around and gave us both a belt to
wear across our middle because she said our
tummies were disgusting and round and sticking out
and we had to learn to suck them in like
real ballerinas do

she was ten and so was i and we were in the cafeteria
and for the first time i watched her stand up and throw
her lunch away and she said it was because she'd eaten
a big breakfast and because i was young, i believed it
and every day since i wish that i hadn't

she was twelve and so was i the first time we went
swimming with guys and we both cackled loudly and
whispered in each other's ears about the things the
older kids talked about and played like we were adults
and i remember being jealous of the way the boys
looked at her but i honestly don't remember ever
seeing her eat during
that whole summer

she was fourteen and so was i and her hair was falling
out and her lips were blue and her eyes were so empty
you could fall into them and we had a sleepover and
she told me, "look, i'm an angel," and stuck out her
shoulder blades like they were wings and i was scared
for her life because i could count every bone in her
spine and could see each of her ribs and i begged her to
get better, i told her,
you promised we'd be best friends forever,
how am i supposed to dance without my partner

but i couldn't help her i didn't know how
and her family
never even knew
because sucking in tummies is
just what
ballerinas
do

she stayed sixteen
and i got older.

i still miss her
every day.

i left my heart
by the side
of her grave.

"I need to look sick and frail and broken so that I look how I feel."

you're going to fall in love with a girl
with hair a little longer than mine,
another writer-type with all sorts of ideas about things
but perhaps a little less aggressive about them, you're
going to kiss her in the ways i taught you and
you're going to figure out some new ways too and
when the two of you have sex, she will be just a little
bit better at it than i ever have been

you're going to fall in love with a girl that smells good
enough you bury your face in the curve of her neck and
her tummy will never growl like
mine always did. she'll be deep and mysterious
but she won't come with the heavy past sitting on her
shoulders. she won't ever keep you awake
with worry. she'll always text you back
and never bite too hard and never act in a way she
can't explain later. she will not cry when she gets
drunk, she'll just fall asleep beside you.

you'll fight with her sometimes because all couples
fight but it won't be with the teeth and claws that we
had, it will be almost gentle,
it will be over before it really gets going

you're going to love her
until you're no longer really sure if what we had
was all that special. you'll start badmouthing me to all
your friends. you'll forget about me in most moments
and eventually you won't even be able to tell someone
what our first date was or our first kiss
or even if you fucked me
the last time that we spoke.

i'll just be gone to you, just a memory of a memory, a girl with dark eyes, a half-capable poet, some word on your tongue you're no longer sure of but you remember that you used to know it.

i will no longer be important.

right now i have two overdue projects that i should be
working on but instead i'm staring at my laptop screen
trying to get up the energy to actually do
anything
but knowing me, i probably won't
until the last possible moment.

right now my stomach is growling and i should be
spending the five bucks my dad gave me for lunch on a
tuna sandwich,
but i won't because
i don't deserve it

right now i just have to open facebook
and send out a message to each of the friends
that i have neglected to talk to
but i won't because
if i disappear
they probably won't notice.

my life isn't awful.
i make it like this.
for some reason,
i make it harder
than it needs to be

and i honestly don't know what's wrong with me.

"My life is not the problem. I'm the problem."

i was four and the waves came
to swallow my sandcastle
and my father told me that there are some things
we cannot save
and i cried

i was seven when i first saw a stranger
seriously injured. blood wept all over her. they pushed
me to the side to help her and i just
stood there and stared

i was fifteen the first time someone finally asked about
the thin red lines and when i told them it was my cat
they just nodded and forgot about it

i am twenty and trying to save everyone who comes
through my life because i was so bad for so long and it
marked me in ways i am still discovering
even though i know all too well
you can't save everyone

since despite all my pretending
i couldn't even
save myself.

"I'm just tired of not being able to fix everything."

no, you don't get it, okay,
it's just like...
fuck.
it's just like.

it's like the future is this lump in my throat i can't
swallow like i bit off more than i could chew and now
it's rotting in my esophagus
and making everything taste bitter;
i mean i can't even like a boy, he's gonna graduate and
we're going to go our separate ways. i can't make
friends, we're all going to different colleges. can't go
to school too far from home without my parents
freaking out, but can't stay here because i hate this
town and the people inside it.
i can't handle the idea of four more years of school and
doing the same shit but in a different setting and with
higher expectations. i can't go to college without
worrying how i'm gonna work with the degree that
follows my passions, can't get into a great school
because my grades are only average,
can't go to an average school because i'm supposed to
be the "perfect" kid that they're proud of, can't really
tell you who i want to be or what i want to be doing
when i'm older, can't get a tattoo at this age
because obviously i'll "regret it forever"
can't really tell you what my dreams are or where
the fuck
i'm going

and i just hate this. i hate not knowing.

"Will I still be able to go to college?"

the problem poets have is that
we really just want to live
inside a poem.

we want our lives to be
like the ink on pages, we want
bruises on our kneecaps
and kisses on our foreheads
so we can have love and pain in equal measures,
to wake up with you making pancakes
in my kitchen,
your bags packed and your hands full
with two plane tickets, i want you to say
"i'm coming with you,
we're going on an adventure"
i want you to be as wild and full of romance as i write
you

but you're a human being and
today i woke up alone
and after a while got a text from you asking
if i still needed a ride to the airport.
there were no flowers when you came for me,
no interfering with the intercom so you could read me
a dumb sonnet you wrote last night
while drunk.
there was only the sound of flights taking off
and lovers kissing each other over and over
until it's kind of awkward
because the goodbye seems to stretch out
over forever
and there was no teddy bear
no promise rings no big

emotional send-off
you just promised to call and gave me a hug

the problem with being a poet
is that you get all sorts of wrong ideas
about what it means to be
in love

because you can hear music
in what sounds like noise to other people,
you crave the kind of flashbang
that your words can create,
you romanticize the ugly because it makes for good
writing and you drain the beautiful until
it comes undone, you forget other people need space to
breathe,
you live in the captured moment of too-perfect
impossibility, you forget that he can't read your mind,
that she doesn't really like your writing, that they
would rather watch sports than go out tonight,
you forget that
most people don't try to make fireworks out of
everyday life,

eventually, after writing more pages about magic
than kisses you've received
you mess up and
actually start to believe.

"I am leaving for Europe and all I can think about is how badly I want you to come with me."

I LOVE YOU AND YOU LOVE
HER.
We are like lighthouses
on opposite shores
and I believe
if you and I
could ONLY CONNECT,
~~~~ WE would outshine
the SUN —/
but we are kept
separate by a
beautiful girl with
eyes like the ocean.

R.I.D

"He lives thirty minutes away from my place, but I can't see him."

Look around your college classroom,
  spot the virgins.

See, this seems like a game until you skip over the girl
  with a short skirt and hair in front of her eyes
  because you heard last summer that she slept with like
  nineteen guys. You can't see her hands, but they're
  under the table, pulling a rosary through her fingers as
  she tries to wash the sin off her. She's only ever kissed
  three people in her whole life and they're all girls. She
  turned down the wrong guy and he told everyone she's
  "a whore." The label "slut" stuck to the bottom of her
  shoe and swallowed her up.

But that quiet girl who is always reading probably never
  touched someone else's penis, you figure,
  because you don't know that she goes home and strips
  down and pulls on tight black leather, you don't know
  she's got a set of whips that could make any set of
  knees quiver, you don't know because she's proud of
  what she does but she's not going to let anyone know
  about it. She's sexy, just not here, not where people
  judge.

See, the truth is: you have no idea who has lost their vir-
  ginity, because it doesn't change you. It doesn't give
  you some kind of glow or superpower or stamp
  on your forehead. You know the feeling of
  waking up on your birthday and thinking "I don't feel
  any older whatsoever"? That's what maybe they're all
  so afraid of you finding out: sex doesn't change you.
  Sex doesn't make you an animal, sex doesn't suddenly
  make your relationship a million times more stable or
  intimate or romantic - it can't fix what's broken,
  although it can make the pain go away for a bit. Sex
  doesn't really occur with eighty tea lights and a thick
  white rug. Sex is ugly and loud and frequently

awkward, sex is excellent and breathtaking and when
you wake up the next morning, you're the exact same
person. There's not some magical connection
with the person in bed beside you. Believe it or not,
pregnancy isn't some kind of punishment - but practice
safe sex, get tested, don't spread your germs around.
They want to tell you, "Sex can ruin you," and I've
heard that a lot as a little girl, that some boy would join
me under my sheets and then dump me four days after,
used, unhappy.

But I figured out that I'm not a fucking toy. Letting
someone have sex with me is not letting them "use"
me, because I'm not an object. My father said the issue
lay in the fact "Men are insecure and need to know that
they're the best you ever had," but I think that's a
steaming crock of absolute bullshit and if I didn't tell
the people I'm with how many others I'd slept beside,
there would be literally no way for them to know my
number, because I don't rust, I don't wear out, I don't
get bruised. I'm not a wilting fruit, I don't go rotten.

But here's the thing: some people connect sex and
emotion. I don't personally because I am probably
secretly an ice storm in disguise, but I still respect my
partner's desires. If they're the type to want love and
sex to coincide, I let them. I don't make fun, I don't
pull one-night-stands or friends-with-benefits, because
it's not their "reputation" I'm afraid for: it's their heart
I'm defending.

Here's the thing: Instead of worrying about people's
"purity" and how it defines them as a person, worry
instead about how you can protect other people's
emotions.

Because here's the thing: look around your room and spot
the virgins. Look harder. You can't tell. Sex doesn't

alter people; it doesn't make them act in a certain way nor dress in a certain manner. Sex and personality have nothing to do with each other. There's a reason that virginity doesn't show on someone's face: because having sex doesn't cause you to change.

"I lost my virginity to a boy I didn't even love."

I want my daughter to shudder when I talk about the time I grew up in. I want my son to say, "Was it really that bad" when I speak about injustice. I want my child to curl up in my lap and whisper, "But people didn't know better back then, right, mommy?"

Because I want to say, "No, they didn't, did they? Things are much better now, though, don't worry."

But I am terrified that if we keep picking our teeth with the bones of our neighbors, there won't even be

a future.

"What do you see the world being like in the future?"

we are unmet but
your smile still makes this class less hellish and

your voice shakes whenever you have to speak up
and your hands tremble when you're asked to
do presentations in front of us and
maybe you don't think you deserve to have
your beautiful opinion heard

but i see how you always have an extra pen for that
one kid who is always losing his and how you
subtly shift your tests so the girl next to you
can see your answers because instead of studying last
night, she was up late
talking her friend down from suicide.

i saw how you gave your last piece of gum to the boy
with dark circles under his eyes who wears long
sleeves no matter how hot it is outside
and i saw you shut up that asshole kid,
just looked at him and shook your head
and he stopped teasing that one girl he hates
for no reason

i might not know you,
but i know that you are kind and i just think
maybe someone should repay you
for every small selfless act you've done

and honestly, i'd be honored to be
that someone.

"I barely know him but he's all I can think about."

I loved you for the cold wind that sang inside of you. It was something otherworldly, being in the middle of that tornado but never quite being touched by the fury. I was your *one exception.* I was your holy, your special girl, the single flower you left standing in the meadow. You were soft around me, suddenly shy, a tempest turned quiet rain

and I loved that. I loved being your home, your silent place, your heart.

I should have never trusted myself to the storm. I should have known.

I should have gone home.

i planted small blue flowers
over where you used to kiss me.

they grew in my bones
and spread over my skin.

i am ashes where used to be a rainforest
before you moved in.

i am fixing memories like tombstones
in between the ivy and the roses

i have become
a haunted garden

i still have not managed
to feel whole again.

"Darkness and the emptiness lingers within us; in spite of the fact we have each other."

Maybe I'm just addicted to heartbreak,
to the storms that could take me,

maybe I love the idea
of being in love
more than anything else, maybe I just
like danger,
kisses that could burn you,
bruises on shins,
maybe I live for the bitemarks
love gives,

maybe it's all how I handle my darkness
because if my mind is focused
on the lips of a lover
whose name I can't quite remember,
on the smell of her perfume, on the
sound of his moans -

then I won't have to remember that
I'm all alone.

"They would completely wreck me but I want them so badly."

you tell me you don't "get" it. your smile curls up at the edges. "Why don't people just be happy?" you ask, sticking your fork into our takeout food box. "It's that simple," you say. I close my eyes and try to explain.

picture the person you hate most in this universe. you hate their crooked smile and their annoying voice and their little habits that get on your nerves. you hate everything they do and everything they are and yet everyone's always talking about how great this person is - as if nobody else can see the things you can. this person makes you mean. this person makes you angry. you're generally kind and nice to everyone else - but it's this one piece of trash you just can't handle.

you are assigned this person as your responsibility. you are in charge of their life and their success. you have to do their homework and get them out of bed and keep their friendships going. you have to make sure their parents are happy and make sure they get to school on time and make sure they fulfill all their extracurricular activities. you have to feed them right and pay attention to their needs, and somehow, despite the fact you hate them, you are told to make them happy.

you don't want to do any of these things.

this person is your archenemy. they're really sweet on the surface, but you know better. they are a liar, a cheat, a cruel person – and still yet you have to put in all of this effort to keep their life moving. you get no reward, nothing.

you know this person doesn't deserve anything they get so when they're happy, you sabotage them.

first it's their homework because it's just not important and nobody notices when they don't turn it in. then it's the clubs they wanted to be in. you're too tired to make them stay after school so you start heading home just so you don't have to deal with it. you stop working so hard on those friendships, start going for days without speaking to anyone. when nobody calls you out for it, you let more and more things slide until the only thing this person has left is their body and themselves. and what do you do when you can't hurt their personal lives anymore?

you hurt them.

the thing is, if you're me, if you're battling the same thing I am - that person I hate so much? that person I have to deal with every single day no matter how hard it gets? that person everyone says "they're so lovely why would you hate them," that person I know should have
nothing,
that person I despise more than I could express?

That person is my own shitty self.

"Is it bad, being depressed?"

he hasn't messaged you.
don't look at your phone.

stop dreaming about him so vividly
that you still taste where his ghosted lips met yours.

don't expect at text back at four in the morning
even if you know he was awake.

stop pining after him.
don't wait.

he doesn't think about you
as often as you think about him

your heartbeat and his
are no longer in sync

he doesn't love you
no matter what you want to think.

"We talked about the future like it's something that we share."

but the love wore off,
didn't it?

i was no longer the heat of early morning showers to
you. you could no longer find me in the night sky. you
could no longer taste me in french toast
and good coffee.

you kissed me with distraction until you didn't kiss me
at all, until i was the light you forgot to turn off before
crawling into bed,
something that kept you awake and you didn't want to
address

i promise i tried to scrape together
as much of a beautiful girl as i could pretend to be but
there isn't much that's actually beautiful
about me

maybe that's why you could
just get up
and leave.

"My girlfriend and I are growing apart."

What if I am too scared to ever kiss you?

What if one day you walk down the hallway and your hand is
in someone else's, what if they are the one to push
back your brown hair and look into those wide eyes
and nibble on the soft curve of your chin;

what if one day we are sitting on the floor of your room and
you are talking about him and I realize that I am out of
time, I am out of opportunities, that out of
my own fear, you will never ever love me -

what if in the late night when I have finally given up on you,
when I am trying to teach myself to be
happy you have someone who makes you smile - what
if then you call me up, drunk, tongue too heavy for
liquor to carry so you slur out that you used to love me
so hard that you had chipped
yourself on the edge of my teeth but were too
convinced that I didn't feel the same way so you pulled
back, trying to salvage our friendship

what if I have to laugh and tell you to go to bed, what if I have
to sit there as you hand the phone over to your
more-sober beau as he chuckles and tells me that he'll
fight me if he has to, what if I have to pretend I am
joking when I say "watch out, I'll destroy you"

what if as the years wear on you never really get around to
breaking up with him, what if I stop being your best
friend when you trade me for him

what if I have to watch you marry him on a day that smells
like cherries and air that is springtime warm and skies
that are so clear you wonder if god distilled the clouds
that day - what if I am up at the altar,
not as your significant other but as one of the
bridal party

what if I lose you no matter what action I take? I either wait to
  break myself later

or break us today.

"I really like my best girl friend but she has no idea. It's been a year and I honestly
don't know what to do."

before you take him from me,
please just:

if he's sad, don't make him coffee,
he prefers tea but he doesn't like to be a burden
so he won't tell you if he's uncomfortable
with something, so try to ask him just to be sure
and don't ever
bring up his ex

      not me,
      i guess,
      now,
      but his other one

he never really healed from what
she did to him so be gentle
and if he suddenly stiffens or goes quiet,
be patient, he'll come back to you if you
are gentle about it

      if you can,
      try not to talk shit about me
      even though you'll want to (don't worry
      i do it too) and one night while drunk
      you might go through my facebook
      at least once but
      please remember we have
      one thing in common:

      the boy we love

before you take him
from me,
before it's
your name he calls out
under those blue sheets
please just

get him that present he
always wanted that i was
too poor to afford, he won't ask directly
so pay attention when he mentions it
casually
and if you can, try to get him to
go out sometimes, when he stays in too much
it gets unhealthy; do me a favor
and support him
whole-heartedly
he's a beautiful, incredible person
and deserves a doting
fanbase;
his passions are his first love
so be prepared for when he
forgets you sometimes, it's okay,
that means he trusts you, and
when he's done, he'll come back;
he's got a great sense of humor
but might torture you with
sixteen puns in a row;
please just

do a better job
making him feel whole
because i wasn't
enough,
you know?

"She loved him and never told him, but I love him unconditionally."

This is a tale of forgiveness. This is the story of
a girl with an "authority problem," c-range student
who could have been a 4.0 if she had just tried hard
enough, darkness boiling under her skin to such a
degree that "personal journal" assignments always
ended in the teacher asking her questions like "are you
okay," but never with a real concern, just professional
double-checking as if reminding her that her left shoe
was untied instead of saying
"it looks like you are unraveling."

This is the story of being under the radar in
every year of school because no matter how good she
got, she was never the best, and no matter how bad her
nights were, in the daytime there were still students
with more shock, more awe, more danger signs
pointing towards their temples. This is a small girl
being constantly overlooked, this is having exactly
eighty-four detentions by the end of her sophomore
year for truancy alone because class for her was an
uphill battle that tasted like sulfur and missed
homework, this is a help-wanted sign pasted across her
report card with every single "unexcused absence" she
spent hiding in the library, trying to convince herself
that next time, she'd show up - this is being
too anxious to fail a class completely, this is being too
sad to ever succeed. This is hating every single
moment she spent within those walls, hating the sound
of chalk and projectors and markers and pens on paper.
This is a girl who in seventh grade and a
serious Catholic asked her God to take her math
teacher's life just so she wouldn't have to face the
overwhelming reality of class the next day, this is not
being ambitious enough for the gifted track despite all
that wasted "potential", this is the story of

being perfectly mediocre and because of that,
always being looked over. This girl is me, twenty, and
going back into the jaws of the lion.

I'm going to be a teacher.

I will never make a child feel like I did. I will
never be the cause of burn scars on brainstems,
I will never make a child think they're stupid or
they're not capable of learning. I will never make them
feel unheard, unwanted, unwelcome. I will see their
warning signs and refuse to let them brush off my
questions. It takes one bad teacher to poison a subject
for a student, and I'm going to do my best to reverse
every pain they've felt. It will not be about lectures or
tests or the state standard. It will be about them, about
their education, about their future. They will be
important to me in the way I never was to anyone else.
They will never feel left out. My class will never come
before their mental health. They will be safe as soon as
they enter my room. This is not a jail cell; it's a hotel, a
haven, a place they can finally leave their home life
behind and relax for an instant.

There will be no under-the-radar children. So
long as I live, I will fight to the death to be sure that
what happened to me never does to my kids. I hate
school, I hate this system. I hate the idea that
not flunking is doing well enough. I hate the idea that
being smart is rewarded with more work. I hate so
much about the politics and the standardization of
education that even my poetry
isn't enough to contain it.

I'm going to teach these kids to fall in love with
learning again. It's not about memorization. It's about
discovery, and it's about time we started teaching
like we have passion instead of adding more

poison, started treating it like a war instead of a profession. These kids are going through hell, so let's give them something to fight with.

4.3.2014

IF I MAILED YOU
ALL MY SECRETS

WOULD YOU KEEP
THEM SAFE
OR USE THEM
AGAINST ME?

r.j.d

"He left me and found someone else."

there's a boat in my front lawn that
only saw the ocean once
and i wonder if she still misses the way
the waves swelled underneath her,
i wonder if the reason she
holds onto rainwater
is because she would rather drown
than rot away on land

this is how it feels to be marked futureless:
like you are a ship among land creatures,
except everyone makes fun of the fact
your only talent is being able to swim

the first time i hear the words
"that's not a real major"
i feel the world is a sinkhole
suddenly rising up to swallow me whole,
i feel my chest collapse, i feel like i will explode
and like i will dissolve
in equal measure

and i laugh and i shrug it off and i say
"yeah, i guess so, huh," when i really mean
to explain "i could do anything but this is what
my heart settled on because the idea of living
in some cubicle setting, the idea of giving up
the love of my life, my talent, my calling
just so people will look at my job title and think
'oh look who makes money'
sounds more like extended suicide
than a lifetime filled with harmony"

because i am a ship, and my talent is in
staying afloat. i do not belong on land
with cars and smog and cities and
"#1 accountant" mugs

my ocean is the one thing
i refuse to give up.

"Follow your North Star, no matter what. It is honestly guiding you home."

166

my phone rang and
for one stupid second
 I thought ~~xxxxx~~ maybe
you were calling me
to say something like,

" I can't get you
out of my head, and
I know this is insane
but can we just talk
until we fall in love"

I thought maybe you had
decided to care, but
it was somebody asking
about the math homework.
I hate that I was
disappointed.

r.i.d

"I want to know you."

She means nothing to him anymore
he swears,
and his words feel hot as they settle
in your hair -
"you aren't her,"
he says
but

when the night settles around you
maybe you can taste her tears on his pillow, maybe
you can smell her shampoo or the sweet soap
she agonized over picking out
just so he'd tell her she
reminded him
of lilacs

maybe at first you feel good, good, good,
you feel chosen, you feel
like you won
but

her ghost has become as familiar to you
as your shadow, you taste her toothpaste and
you hear her laughter,
he says "she used to paint her nails like you"
and you say
"yeah?" and
go home
and don't cry, don't cry, don't cry

because he says
you're his and you feel good, good, good

god did he just choose you because you wear her
dresses and like the same things as she did except

you're more into his tv shows and less into weddings
are you just a replacement are you just scar tissue to
fill up the wounds she left are you just the girl between
the girl he wanted to marry and the girl he actually
will

and he says
"she means nothing to me anymore"
and you say
"yeah?"
and some sad sick part of you
knows you should save yourself the trouble
of a heartbreak so loud your neighbors would call the
cops, thinking they heard gunshots

you've seen how these things go:
one day he's going to say
"she meant nothing to me, anyway"
and he'll be talking about
you

you already mean less to him
than you really should

but god help you,
every time he kisses you,
you feel

good, good, good.

"I love him but he still loves her."

YOU WERE A NATURAL DISASTER AND I WAS UNTOUCHED LAND. YOU LEFT ME WITH MORE TORN SKIN THAN ANY ACCIDENT. YOU WERE THE WORST THING THAT COULD HAPPEN, AND SOMEHOW THE BEST ONE TOO. THE MORE TIME THAT I SPEND PICKING UP WHAT YOU RUINED, THE MORE THAT I REALIZE I CAN DO THIS ON MY OWN. THAT MY VOICE IS A SHOUT, NOT A WHISPER. YOU ARE NOT MY EVERYTHING. YOU ARE NOT MY HOME. YOU ARE NOT MY KNIGHT IN ARMOR. I AM A WILDFIRE, I BREAK THE SOUND BARRIER, I SING SONGS, I LIVE LIKE A THUNDERCLAP. I AM SO MUCH STRONGER THAN I EVER KNEW. I AM FINALLY FREE. I NEVER NEEDED YOU.

"Will I heal from the heartbreak he gave me?"

i. there are more pizza boxes here than home-cooked meals. your friends grab a slice and call you lucky. there are no good memories.

ii. you stay over at a friend's house and marvel at the comfortable silence. nobody argues. there are no unsaid words hanging in the air with the weight of dead men. it is bliss.

iii. the waiter asks, "will that be all?"
and before you can answer, your mother says,
"she's on a diet, so yes,"
and you blush deep wine red.
they do not let you eat ice cream
without making comments.
you can't look at certain foods
without a panic in your chest.

iv. "it's so nice that your parents never talk to you and just leave you alone."

v. where do you go when your house isn't home?

"I'm never having kids. I'm scared of ruining them like my parents did to me."

She called those who commit suicide cowardly and
I couldn't breathe for a second because

In the bathtub of a hotel room, a 4.0 student broke
open her veins and planted death where the skin split
and lay with her head
as far under the water as it could get but
the fear of the end
got too be too strong and she called for help and
it was cowardice that saved her, wasn't it;

in the living room of his rich parents,
the football star sits and stares at the gun in his hands
and thinks about just clicking
the bullet into place
and finally getting this all over with but
he can't stop wondering if this is
really for the best, he can't
stop the panic that rises when he thinks
about the blackness,
he can't stop the thought of
making his girlfriend cry until she collapses -
so he puts the gun down and leaves it, carries the idea
of how incredibly soft he must be
if he couldn't just do that one last thing

I am more grateful to fear than I am to any other
emotion. It has stopped the untimely end of so many of
my loved ones. It has been the only wall between them
and a headstone. It has been proof they are
unfinished

it is their body rejecting the idea that they are
unworthy, that there is such a thing as being "ready"

because that fear? That fear is not failure. That fear is
your heart, still beating, that fear is your lungs, still

breathing, that fear is your bones, still ready to pick
you up from the bottom and carry you to safety, that
fear is your entire system rejecting the idea that you
are unable to survive any longer, that fear is the primal
part of your brain
echoing through your nervous system
just one whisper of desperation:

Stay. Stay. Stay.

You are still capable of so much and so many good
things. That fear is your heart, and she is waiting for
you to remember love. That fear is your lungs, and
they are still filling with hope every time you
inhale. That fear is your bones and your skeleton, and
he is so happy that you are the soul
that came to inhabit him. You are electricity, you are
synaptic connections, you are a beautiful creation
of science and heaven, you are human - and some
part of you wants to stay here, on this good earth
where grass is still green and the sun still makes
freckles on the faces of the people who turn to her and
the moon still makes sure you're tucked in sleeping
and cities are still full of people kissing and
you are still
capable of dreaming

so take the biggest risk there is:
put down the blade, my love,
go out and live.

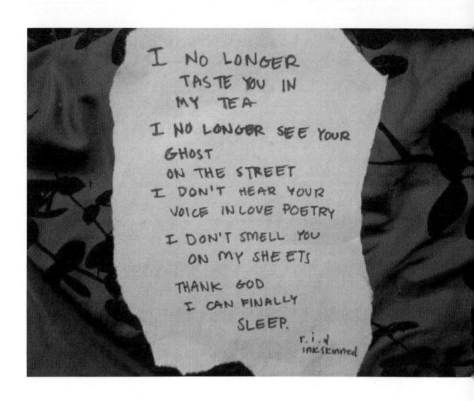

"I think I'm over him finally."

what high school was for me:

– the drowning girl is crowned prom queen
and she's too pretty to be hurting
– the hockey star is swallowing more liquor than his
liver can handle but nobody ever checks on him
because boys don't flounder
– the kid at the back of the class just wants a friend
but thinks it's too much to ask
– the unnoticed ones go through their lives wondering if
maybe they've already died
– everyone believes that if you're not perfect
you're a piece of shit

what high school shouldn't be:

kids living life as if they are constantly flinching,
surrounded by the gunshot echo of their insecurity,
always moving like they are headed towards slaughter,
walking the line between
beautiful success and ugly mistake,
always darting between being a disaster
or getting saved,
either getting a degree
or getting put
in a grave.

"High school was a prison."

It is three o'clock in the morning and I am kept awake by the three thousand reasons I still love you. Every time i close my eyes, another memory plays in front of me like a flash of lighting. i am kept stormcloud by you.

It is three o'clock in the morning and the only way I could write this poem was by waiting until I was sleep-drunk enough to be honest. I want to pick up the phone and call you just to see if you would answer. I want to text you all three thousand reasons that seem so obvious to me, an ever-expanding list of why you feel more like home than the heartache of the building I grew up in, why there's no such thing as kissing you too often, why my palms feel empty when you're not there to hold me, why i crave you like a bullet hole or a speeding train but

it was three o'clock in the morning when you met her. We were all tipsy on more shots than our parents would have been proud of, you were too drunk to notice that fate had tied nooses around our necks, i was too drunk to believe that this could really end. I remember her humor the most, the way her words seem to flow in the moment, the way she filled up a room like she was unafraid of being noticed. later you would curl up beside me with your familiar body heat and you would say "she's funny," and i would pretend to be asleep.

like galaxies with linked arms the two of you fell into an orbit I was not a part of. her laughter followed you home. i could hear her in your heartbeat because it suddenly sounded happy. when i first saw you texting her in the middle of our dinner, you said, "she's great," and I said nothing.

i don't know exactly when but i lost you. maybe it was somewhere between the unanswered messages and forgotten dates and times where the silence between us suddenly felt foreign. maybe it was while i was in the middle of a sentence and you turned up the radio because it was her favorite song. maybe it was the first time you met her.

i watched myself disappear to you. my mother raised me to be titanium, steel plating around soft body, but you were cold diamond and good lord did you cut me. i emptied myself into everything i could. i slimmed down and talked less and didn't ask for anything. i hollowed out, i became two dimensional, i became the sound that fills a room when a song is done. i am a creature of words and i taught myself to live in silence.

it's three in the morning and the last thing you said to me was that you were going to hang out with her. i haven't checked up on you all night. i'm worried about what will happen if i do.

i have three thousand reasons why i love you but yesterday when i asked why you stayed with me, your mouth dried up. she called you before you could answer. i watched your frown melt
at the sound of her voice.

it's three o'clock in the morning and i love you but to you, i mean nothing.

"You cheated with my best friend."

when she found out
that you had left
she gave me
this long sad look,
leaned in
and said

"really, darling,
what did you
expect?"

"He left me and I don't blame him."

it's 3:42 in the morning and i want to text you and pour
out my soul and say, "amen i miss you like a bullet
hole" but the truth is that i miss who you were and
what we had and neither of those things is coming
back and even if i was to call you right now
it wouldn't change anything because
you've become a stranger to me and
the person i love doesn't exist anymore and the
happiness we shared might as well have been a dream
because

even though you have his smile and his laugh and the
way he always runs his hands through his hair:
it's all completely wrong

somehow, the boy i love
is here and also
gone.

their eyes sat like needles on my skin
so when i took a deep breath i was
punctured to my marrow with it

i want to say i'm sorry for how tight my chest gets
whenever there are strangers in my presences or for
how i shake almost always
or for how i ended up
scorching your skin
with the fever heat of my worry

i know i let something beautiful go
but i was surrounded by wasps and their mouths
were all full of knives and i could hear them say
i don't deserve you
even though they never spoke a word;
somehow, even when they were gone,
in the night their voices followed me home,
each of them asking why i was keeping you hostage,
why i subjected you to having to be with me, why i
don't just give it up and
give you back

i let you go because i
love you,
i hope you can see that.

"Me and her broke it off because too many people were on my back."

in sixth grade someone told me that my crooked
glasses made me look even uglier than i already was so
i begged my mom to buy me contacts even though our
bills were tight
and even though the first few pairs made me dizzy;
funny thing is that afterwards everyone admitted
one by one
that they had kind of hated
what i looked like beforehand
so i just smiled and said
absolutely nothing

in eighth grade i lost ten pounds over the summer and a
pretty girl told me that if i kept it up one day i could
actually be attractive
in tenth i cut off my beautiful long hair after a boy
broke my heart and my teacher said,
"thank god that's gone,"

in junior year after someone made a comment about
how mannish i am, i started wearing a dress every day
no matter how cold i was and about eighty people told
me, "you look so much better in those"
and this whole time
i just smiled and said
absolutely nothing

in senior year while my best friend and i were driving,
i mentioned that i no longer wanted a tattoo because
someone else had said that i already stick out like a bad
wound, i said i didn't want to add to that sort of
attention
and she yanked the wheel the side, pulled us over,
her hair a mess while she whispered,
"who the fuck have you become,"

and i looked straight ahead and smiled and said,
"absolutely no one."

"*It's so hard to love yourself when everyone else is trying to change who you are.*"

I was six when Robert from down the block
pushed me onto a pile of rocks.
my mama brushed the dirt off my cheeks,
washed off my bleeding knees
and told me, "don't cry, don't show
weakness"

in fifth grade my friend's cousin passed away and
two days later i overheard some boys
calling her a crybaby

i think maybe i complain a lot about small things
like sore joints or headaches or chapped lips or
how long it is until the next episode of game of
thrones

so everyone thinks the only problems in my life
are itty bitty butterflies but
I don't talk about the bad stuff;
you know? I don't mention
the stuff that's
eating me up, the stuff that makes this skin

feel less like home and more like a prison,
the stuff that's making my particles disconnect
from one another so i become
atomic dust, i just

i help a lot of people with their burdens,
as often as i can and i know logically
they wouldn't really mind it if i told them maybe
just a little about how bad it's getting

but even my closest friends
i never want to bother because i hear their stories

about what they're carrying and
i don't want to add to it
when they're sad enough as it is
and when they're happy, I know exactly
how rare it is for them,
so I don't want to spoil it

the only thing is
a few days ago, I offered advice
to someone who needed a pick-me-up
and she looked me in the eyes and asked
"how is it exactly that you know this stuff"

and I could have unzipped my bones and come
crashing out all over the floor

but instead I shrugged and smiled and said
"That's just what I do. It's what I'm here for."

"I think I'm depressed. Or burdened. Or something. I can't get my shit straight. I am always looking for somebody to fix. Or save. Or shape into a butterfly."

i.   the first time one of my friends tried to commit
suicide, i was thirteen. they kept her in the hospital for
two days. when we found out she'd swallowed tylenol
in excess to get all her pain to stop, some dudes made a
comment about how she was trying too hard, how if
she'd really wanted it she would have sucked down
bleach instead. behind her back, her failure wrote itself
into a punchline. i felt each joke like a crack against
my own bones. i didn't speak up. i didn't know how.

ii.   the first time i met you, your eyes danced with enough
light that i think you made the sun jealous. we grew up
as garden children, soft soil bodies that only wanted to
erupt with flowers instead of bruises. you were the
only person who read my poetry without laughing or
saying it was too dark to be good. you were the only
one who told me i should keep on writing.

iii.   the first time someone in my school died, i watched
girls collapse in the hallways crying. teachers
cancelled classes. we wore black armbands.
everyone talked about how unfair it was. everyone
talked about themselves.

iv.   the first time i told someone about the cuts was
in the eighth grade. she didn't believe me. she laughed
at the idea.

v.   the last time i told someone about the cuts was in the
eighth grade. i never recovered. i'm twenty-one.

vi.   the last time i saw you, there was a smile on your face
and your eyes were the Northern Lights. you and i held
hands and ran through the rain and shook our fists at

the sky and curled under blankets and told each other secrets. we were almost asleep when you said you wanted to die.

vii. i still visit your grave from time to time.

"I lost her to suicide and I still write her occasionally. It's been almost four years but it still hurts like hell some days."

you looked like heaven
but tasted like destruction.

you broke me open.

"I fell for a boy who pretended to care for me. I didn't think he would end up meaning anything to me but I was wrong."

He is missing first from your facebook page when five minutes after the phone call ends, you see it on your newsfeed: the boy you love is recently single and six people have already liked it. That's it. You're officially over. You feel an odd lurch in your stomach as if you are at the top of a roller coaster. Your cheeks warm and your breathing comes faster. Something inside of you beats like fists against your skin, his words like bruises inside of your bones.

The next morning you wake up and almost text him good morning but remember at the last second that you no longer can, and for some reason
the inside of your brain
becomes a rainstorm.

He becomes a vast, throbbing emptiness in your life. He is absent from hello hugs and last-minute kisses and homework complaints and making rude faces at each other in the hallway. He is gone from your bed and your future, and yet your heart has not forgotten him.

You cannot bring yourself to erase your text conversations. Every time you reread them, your wounds sear wide open. You cannot get rid of the way he tasted and now your coffee reminds you of his kisses. You hear him in lyrics and in poetry and see him in romantic comedies and it almost makes you sick for it, sick for the absence of something that used to take up so much space in your life that you had built dreams on the foundation of thinking he'd be there to see them.

He's just gone. Even though every little thing reminds you of him, even though your weak heartstrings still cling with tired desperation, even though the want of him is still a solar flare in your palms: he's gone completely. You want to ask him if it was easy, sweeping you out of his braincave - but something tells you that you'd only end up crying, choking on the letters as they fell to pieces, trapped in the same mouth that used to nibble on his collarbones.

Something tells you that no matter how wide and brilliantly painful it is for you, it has touched him none at all. Something tells you that even if you showed up drunk on his doorstep with every memory the two of you shared clutched in your cold fingertips, he'd turn you away in an instant.

Because that's the thing, isn't it?

He has completely erased you from his life while you can't stop loving him.

"When you left, I tried so hard to forget."

This is a confession: I didn't really want to go to your birthday party.

I know that the summer sun treats you well but short sleeves and I don't usually like each other and besides you're always the most important person at every event and always talking to a million other people other than me and I just have to stand there and force a smile while patiently waiting the appropriate amount of time before I can make an excuse and leave so instead of being as pumped up as you were I kind of just sighed and steeled myself for
another loud and awkward night

but it turned out to be pretty quiet and you and I got nicely tipsy without anyone trying to get us to chug things and we sat on your swingset and talked about the good times and you leaned your head on my shoulder and said "Thank god you came. I love everyone but they wear me out. You're my only real friend, you know?" and I think those words got me higher than any drug ever could because I couldn't stop smiling for days after.

This is a confession: I think that was the night I started to fall in love.

This is a confession: The times when I turned you down and told you I was too tired to go to the movies were usually because I'd been up all night trying to figure out what the fuck was going on in my heart because more and more often I'd find myself stuck on the idea of you as if you were a thorn except the pain was kind of good but at the same time laced with guilt I mean you were my friend and if this was just some dumb crush I could get over it and it wouldn't even effect what we had but what if it got bigger inside of my chest because if it did then I was really in for trouble since that meant I could actually mess things up between us; so yes every time you asked me "do you wanna hang today," the answer was always "absolutely," but half the time I had to be like, "no say no give yourself time to get over this." it never really worked but I felt like a better friend.

This is a confession: I drop everything I'm supposed to hold onto tight but for some reason no matter how hard I tried I couldn't lose my grip on you.

By the time we'd spent a year just being best friends I had figured out that maybe I just felt deeper about you than anyone else only because you were the sun to me, you were the reason that I'd be happy, you were what I was looking forwards to no matter what else I had that day so I just assumed maybe that's what close friends do but

one day you left on vacation and for a solid two weeks I didn't hear from you because neither of us could afford the roaming charges and those two weeks basically defined everything for me because I'd missed people before but this was nothing like that, this was as if I was missing my other half and when you came back the first and only thing I wanted was to kiss you like crazy and while we were hugging I realized just how fucked I was because my only thought was to say, "I missed you, my love" and in that moment I wished so hard we were something more than just being good friends I almost broke my own heart for it and

This is a confession: I don't hug you anymore because I think it's unfair to you because it means so much more to me. I don't jokingly say, "I love you, babe," because I'm afraid my voice will crack and when the words hit the air they will ring with truth. I don't say stuff like "honey" or "sweetheart" or "darling" around you because you've always been able to read me like a book and maybe one of these pet names will actually show you what you mean to me.

This is a confession: I didn't even want to go to your birthday party. I didn't want to fall in love with you. I didn't want to fuck this up because it's the most important thing in my life and when I inevitably ruin it with my stupid brain and stupid crush and stupid need for you, it's gonna break me. And last night when we were both drunk and laughing and you were lying beside me I was so close to telling you the truth that I started shaking and when later you whispered, "confess something," I almost snapped like a twig into tiny pieces and instead just started laughing and made up something like, "I failed my last test," but

This is my confession: I'm never gonna tell you any of this.

"I think I'm in love with my best friend."

i just have bad habits i guess
like i chew on my nails no matter how old
i get and i know it makes me look thoughtless
but wait until you see how often
i gnaw on my lips
because i'm basically addicted
maybe i'm just trying to tear off the
last bits of skin
that felt your kiss

and sometimes i take cold showers
or refuse to towel off and even though
i hate not being warm it's because
my brain gets stuck on some ideas like
burning a few extra calories without
trying very hard
kind of like how it got stuck on the idea
that you might still love me even after
all the pretty
wore off

and i have a habit of panicking about times
like i can't be late to anything
or my body becomes
an explosion and my words become
frozen
you were the first person i would have rather spent
those five extra minutes with like i would have
shown up late to everything if it meant
just a couple continued moments of us
lying quiet in our bed

and i like reading more than some people and
i will try to pet every dog i come across
and i am just really awful at crossing streets

like for no reason my timing with that is actually
horrifying and i like to touch every water feature
around me even if it's in some highclass lawyer place
where they frown at you
for running your fingers across their wall fountain and
occasionally i spend
like an embarrassing amount of time in my pajamas
and i always procrastinate no matter what i have
for homework and i also have this thing where
i second-guess everything i do

but by far my worst habit
is not being able
to stop loving you.

"He left without a reason or saying goodbye, and now I can't breathe."

193

i am jealous of the dying sun.

every day
the clouds and i bear witness
as the sky swells with the
wet red artwork
of her blood

i wish i could be as she is:
to come back every morning

no matter how many times
she kills herself
with the blade
of our horizon.

"I hate myself a little more every day."

it's just
you said you'd listen to my story
after you were done on the phone but
when i came back you asked what was
"so goddamn important"
i couldn't stop nagging you about it
and since it was something stupid that
i had just hoped
would make you laugh
i told you to forget about it

it's just
you said you'd read my writing and
not make fun of it but in reality
i've never stopped being a joke in this family
because in middle school i wrote dark short stories
where the main character died and yeah in
retrospect
maybe that's funny but
there's also a reason why since then i don't
show you anything
because at thirteen hearing you refuse to take my work
seriously
didn't really make me feel like laughing

it's just
you said that school was important but
at the same time would get so pissed at me
if i stayed up doing homework
all i would hear is
"why didn't you start this
earlier"
and when i tried to explain

i had other things to do, i was told "i don't want to hear
it, just get it done"
and if i ever mentioned that i was stressed to the point
of breaking into glass pieces
you always rolled your eyes
and said "you don't even
know what stress is,"
even though when i asked for help on projects
you'd barely even look at it before
deciding it was too difficult

it's just
you've never said
that you're proud of me
only told me the things i should be fixing
like how i'm kind of getting a tummy
and my hair is always messy and how
i'll never get married if i don't start
being more mature and
how i need to work on being the perfect student or
i'll never amount to anything
and i need to patch up my personality
i don't know but
when you asked me why i've been
"so distant lately it's kind of bitchy"
i got as far as

"it's just"
before you said
"don't start with me."
i don't know what you want. i wish i could just
leave.

"Are your parents supposed to make you hate yourself?"

We are young, our love is raw the way
sunburns feel in showers, our love
is over concentrated
so the smallest drop
could kill a person, our love
is branded unsafe for consumption because

our love is quickfire and risky and unbiased
and as soon as it comes
it's gone

we are stamped with expiration dates because
kids get older and magic doesn't always hold on
one day, time will make this all go wrong
and our lives
will get in the way
the lines will all get crossed

maybe that's the reason that when we love,
we love twice
as strong.

"'Forever' is a silly thing to say by someone as young as we are, but it's kind of what I want with him."

see
it's funny

like how my friend of five years
sent me a video where a man fakes the suicide
of his friend's girlfriend
as just a prank

"this is brutal," said my friend, "but it's
so fucking hilarious"
and it was, it was
funny

funny like how i'm still picking the bone shards
of my first boyfriend's death out of my system,
funny like how the razors weighs nothing at all but at
the same time feels like a brick in my palm,
funny like i lasted six days without food before
i fainted on a staircase and when i woke up
my first thought was that i was weak and
six days was not enough
funny like how clothes cover scars but you have to
learn how to keep your face from showing how
mismatched your pieces are
funny like shaking fingers, bruises knees,
anxiety's dragon breathing fire down
your brainstem

funny like death, like
gallows humor,
funny like i hide it all
because people don't like burdens
and my life
is a joke.

"I didn't want to be 'that girl who cuts'."

i mean half the time i want someone to notice
but the minute someone asks about the burns
or the cuts
suddenly i kind of shut down
and feel a lie crawling out of my throat

maybe it's because the people who point it out
somehow are never the ones i'm closest to
maybe it's because we all want to believe
the best possible things about each other
and all my friends want to think i'm happy,
to think my brain is healthy and tonight
i'm going to bed early instead of
battling the desire to pull my last razor
from where i hid it and to relapse to a degree
that would make my soul shake; the problem is
i hear the voices tell me
"give up now, you will anyway,"

i mean i know my friends love me or at least
that's what they say
but even though i've had to blame everything
from my cat to a falling box to a bike accident,
even though i hate lying to them
and know they're good people and
probably want to help,
for some reason i have
never
told them i feel this way

half of me wants to die
and the other half
wants saving.

"I feel like I'm slowly rotting inside every day, even when I smile to hide it. I hate myself."

you should probably run from me now
and save us both the time and heartbreak

i'm kind of broken but in an ugly way
and without me wanting it
my insecurities will run tests on you,
waiting for proof you don't love me
like you say you do

i'll say i don't care about compliments but if i spend
five hours getting ready and you don't mention it,
suddenly i feel this crushing weight in my chest
and while the logical parts of me know you were
probably just waiting for the right moment or gathering
your words or something,
for some reason i break anyway,
decide you don't like me

i'm just oversensitive or too attached
or just really fucking bad at telling you what i need
since i hate sounding that clingy
and who wants to date someone
who is constantly asking if you don't secretly want
to break up, who is always checking to see
if you really mean it
no matter how much work you put into
our relationship

i don't even know
how i am supposed to believe
you want to hang around me,
despite everything else

when i can't even stand myself?

"I can't believe you love me."

you only cry at the thought of losing her
when her fingers have grown weak
from holding you two together and
she needs to leave for
her own good

you only remember
she's the most beautiful girl in the room
when she's alone

you only remember how sweet her lips are
when you're filled with fireball or
she's laughing at someone else's jokes

you only want to kiss her to possess her
the way a dog protects his bone

you only miss her
when the night gets dark around you
and your empty bed feels cold

you only fill up her fingers with yours
when it looks like she'll find another hand
to hold

you only love her when "yes" turns into "no"

only want her to stay
when it looks like she might
go.

"He says he cares but never shows it. I love him too much to be unscathed."

people just
fall for her
effortlessly

she has this way
of sticking in your brain,
so you can't quite
pick her out of your skin,
she's the whole garden,
a perfect diamond

and i'm just a simple
dandelion.

if she makes you happy, i guess i can
sit with her at lunch and laugh over
a bowl of salad or something,
be nice to her, be her friend,
try not to compare myself to
what she is

i just
love you more than
window panes love ultraviolet rays
they catch every single one and hold on,
vibrate at the same frequency, are
perfectly matched to one another

and sure yeah maybe
it chokes me
to think of you in the arms of someone else

with your lips on her skin,
your laughter pouring out to answer
her jokes, your smile following her
wherever she goes,
your soul in her safekeeping,

her name on the back of your tongue

but if you really love her and she's your
one,

i promise i will try
to make her feel welcome.

"He has a girlfriend."

i think of the way your eyelashes looked while
your smirk played around the edges of the straw
when, just because it made me laugh,
you tried the cheap iced coffee
that i put too much sugar in
and your cheeks sucked inwards at
the sickening sweetness

i think of waking up from cold nightmares
to find that you are warm beside me,
your freckled skin
no more than six inches from mine
and most nights i had to ask you to
please move over because while you slept
your body would follow me across the bed
and this
unconscious chasing
made me happier than i ever said

i think of how everything grew softer
when you were there,
how the moments that should have broken me
were only a little stormy and how
the moments that were overly romantic we could laugh
about but still enjoy and
i think about how it felt every time i remembered that
you were mine,
this odd rush of joy and pride,
i think about how
the light played across you
and how you sounded singing along at concerts and
the slight flush you'd get when tipsy and

how easily you fit into my soul as if you'd always
been the right piece

it's okay.
you must have not felt the same
about me.

i hope she makes you feel
complete.

"I still love him but he moved on. Maybe I should move on too."

you grew flowers in my veins
where i tasted only iron

i became
a garden

you found angels in my shoulder blades
where i had only felt fallen

you are forests and i am
the bleak desert sun

i only ever learned
how to burn someone.

"I'm scared I'm falling in love with you so quickly."

your lips never unlearned her name
as if she had tattooed herself inside your teeth.
you dream about her,
cry her name in your sleep

she is the summer rain and
her smile is so quick maybe that is why
it still feels like lightning as it runs up
your veins

but you are blackmoon nights
where you chew off your fingernails and
start fights with too much alcohol
to see who winds up empty:
you or the bottle

so you let her go because waterlilies
don't call deserts like you
a home

he better know the measure
of the girl he wraps his arms around
because oh god oh fuck oh sweet lord
if she is a skyscraper,
you are just dirt

and you will do
anything
to make her
the happiest girl
in this world.

"My best friend loves me dearly, but I'm already in a relationship with someone."

i love you i just wish
remembering you
and remembering
what we had

     didn't make me
     so fucking

          sad.

"I thought she loved me."

i am stones
where used to be cities;
if you breathe too close
you can still smell
burning

i am a shell
constructed from
illusion and poetry

but you
are the kind of person
who sees galaxies
in your coffee
where others just see
sugar and cream
and you're the one who says,
"go on, i'm listening"
no matter how boring my story is,
you're who makes sure i get home safe,
that i'm eating well, that i'm
doing okay

you must be
an archeologist
because where others saw
chaos and
spite

you looked into my eyes
and whispered,
"you're so full of life."

"He always said I didn't love him. I do."

i have seen girls
that are trapped in windowless rooms
with a boy who only kisses them back when
his lips taste of liquor
and neither of them can admit
their love is over

i have seen boys
head over heels
for someone who cannot get up the effort
to say hello to them

i have seen people
wreck themselves
on the sharp parts of love

what if in two weeks or two months
or two years
that's us

what if we pass through a storm and
on the other side, what we thought was open road
is just soot, what if i am pollution,
what if while we are discussing my favorite movie
i realize you and i are not a perfect fit

what if i only feel like you're my everything
right in this minute

i don't want to look back on these
beautiful days

only to see
it was all a mistake.

"What if we don't work, and we just quietly fall apart?"

we crossed a bridge with riverwater sleeping under
a fog bank and as the car purred forwards
i dipped my hand into the current of the air
and happened to catch the reflection of my wrist
in the side mirror for a second

and for a brief second
i looked skinnier than i was used to seeing
and it hurt me

i tried to explain to him
that the scariest part of this
was never actually knowing what i
really looked like

but those sorts of things
don't make sense to other people

they only see
who they are
in the mirror.

i don't know, i'm sure i seem vain,
always staring at my reflection
but most of the time i can't understand it's
me living inside that body.
i'm trying to figure out exactly what it is
that other people see

i keep looking to see if one day it shows
that i don't feel whole

i keep looking to see if one day, i see
my soul.

"Everyone says how pretty I am and how much they want to be like me. But why can't I believe them?"

Stage One: You only trust others in the way small animals trust humans: you take flight as often as you can and leave them with the taste of feathers in their mouths. You do not bring people to where the nest of your heart is, others do not get access to where the broken eggshells of your soul lay scattered around. Instead you are bright white smiles and laughter and a wit so sharp a lover could cut themselves on it. This is a mask so well-fit that recently one of your friends said, "You're like the happiest person I know," and you didn't even flinch.

Stage Two: They somehow stay around long enough that they notice your wings are clipped and you limp when you walk. They ask and you give answers that sashay away: "It was a long time ago," "Don't worry about it," "You should see the other guy." They can smell the blood but they don't know where it's leaking from. You are learning to let them in but goddamn it's dark in here and you know better than to turn on the lights so they stand on your front porch and knock at your door and you pretend you're not home. You say to yourself:
"they just think I'm broken and they're looking for someone to fix they have no idea how bad it is."

Stage Three: in the back of class or before a movie or in the middle of the woods, you slip up and they see it. it's always something different. sometimes they catch the way your eyes turn dead when you think nobody is looking, sometimes it's your sleeves riding up, sometimes it's the untouched lunch. they bring it up or maybe they don't but it kills you that they know. a lot of them ask if you're okay and you say "yeah, of course" and then that's the last you talk of it.

Stage Four: for some reason, they stick around even though your presence is poison and slowly staining them. they become your lighthouse, your breadcrumbs, your way home. you think maybe it's time to open up but when you do, invariably you're drunk or high or dead tired because even though you love them you would never be in your right mind to admit to the demons. you spill out of your outline, just a little at a time. they learn you, they watch you, they keep you sane, and then in the late night, you finally make that mistake and fill their ears with your story from start to finish and have to deal with the look that crosses their faces.

Stage Five: I actually don't know what it's like to be with someone who knows all of you and yet doesn't leave. If you find out, please get back to me.

"I told him everything about my past. He promised he would be different from the rest; he wouldn't leave. I can feel him distancing himself from me. They never are different."

1. When he starts distancing himself from you, do not restring bridges with your own sinew. You will find yourself two months later coming unraveled, coming undone. You will find he has left you in the places he has visited and in the hair of the girls he has imagined kissing. You will find yourself splatterpainted on the walls where while drunk he confessed all of your secrets to his college friends. You will be crying on the floor, surrounded by the parts of you he has stepped on, and he will look you in the eyes and ask you to clean up the mess.

2. When she cannot get through the words "I love you" without her eyes flicking to the side or her tongue slurring or her mouth pressing in at the edges: do not assume it is your fault. Do not think that you have yet again pushed away someone amazing. You have not. Sometimes people knock on their bones and find themselves hollow. You were the only way they felt momentarily whole, do not empty yourself to fill up their soul. Do not shatter into pieces trying to perfect yourself. You do not need to be glass to turn light into rainbows. You are a person, not their prism.

3. Do not let them hold you against their body if you know they do not cherish every second they are in contact with your skin. I know it feels as if you are breaking your own spine, but tear yourself away from them. Know that the something beautiful you had was already fading. Know that in the end you did the only thing you could. Sometimes people grow apart. Even trees do it.

4. Cry. Want them back.

5. Cry. Do not take them back.

6. In the following months, you will rediscover what it means to be alone. You will sit and stare at a ceiling and hate yourself and hate the world and cry about everything because everything hurts. You will wonder if it could have gotten better if you'd just been a little different, if the timing had worked out, if, if, if. Do not worry about this.
Nothing would have changed the reality that the person you were in love with had stopped loving you somewhere along the line, whether it was in the middle of a conversation or while driving under a bridge or when they made eye contact with someone new and wonderful. It doesn't matter. Stop wasting your time on them. You don't need to stop your story just because they are no longer a main character. Do not take back what has already poisoned you. Instead start healing and start healing soon.

7. Take yourself back. Bring out the mop, the broom, the magic wand. Glue where needs to be glued, put up new paint, turn off the lights in places that are too hot to touch. Touch your toes. Touch your hair. Touch a dog. Touch the grass, touch the telephone, do not call him. Touch base with your mom. Touch another person with no love in your heart,
touch another person and mean every second of it. Believe in yourself even if you don't believe in love. It's okay. There is nothing wrong with being alone. You are the best company you'll ever know. It's okay. It's okay. You're gonna be okay and none of this was ever your fault. Sometimes people just fall out of love. It's okay. It's okay. You'll one day discover you didn't need them anyway.

"How to stop loving someone who does not love you."

thank god for the soap in my eyes,
for the torn contact lenses,
scraped knees,
paper cuts,

for thorns in my heels,
splinters under fingernails,
bee stings,
mosquito bites

somewhere inside each little arc of pain

i was alone for an instant.
no thoughts of you plagued me.

for one second,
i could just

be.

"Last night he told me that he doesn't love me anymore and that he outgrew me."

my papa tells me,
"go out and get a boyfriend,"
probably somebody with eyes like a wasp
that sits around the house instead of cleaning
who goes bald by thirty

but papa

her eyes are clearer than poetry and i think my ears are
addicted to how she sings in the shower while water
holds her curves the way my fingers want to
and i'm obsessed with how
she'll laugh while kissing you because she just thought
of a joke she heard
i mean she lets me cook dinner even when i burn it and
when she curls up next to me i finally feel like i'm
home

maybe we don't have much
but our love is a running start

and maybe she's not good in a fist fight and
can't tune a car

but papa i swear

she sure as hell fixed my heart.

"I think about her every day."

you left me so suddenly
that the insides of me felt scraped clean
and i was trying to stitch myself together with
shaky hands and bad dreams and

i was so
fucked up about it
one night even though i don't ask for things
i texted you and begged you
to please come back because
everything reminds me of the way
that you feel and you told me
"go write some of that awful fucking
poetry you never left me out of
why not write about this heartbreak
at least it's something new"

but lord have mercy;
no matter how hard i bite down
even these words
taste of you.

"I fell in love with a guy who didn't give a shit about me."

i came to you when i was still chewing on the graphite
of another boy's poems, still drowning in the
ink splotches he left along my collarbones, still
flinching every time someone raised their voice and

the first time we talked it scared me how easily i could
fold myself into your sentences and the first time we
got drunk together i remember lying beside you just
barely touching and still feeling like maybe i belonged
here for the rest of eternity

how did you take a girl with a heart so black she
couldn't get it to beat how did you make her finally
feel complete?

you eased open the places i was hurting and
cut yourself removing all of my thorns and i am a
tinderbox and ready to catch on fire but you're the only
person who has ever made me feel warm so

just know that where you are

is where i am home.

"This is the longest relationship I've ever had. I truly hope this one will last."

maybe he was just born on a night where
they left the windows open and a storm
crept into his soul because now he is all
bad dreams and tornadoes, he is sitting on your
front step and lighting a cigarette even though
he would never let you touch one because
"they'll kill you," he said,
he is leaning back on his elbows and
giving you that crooked smile that
reminds you of an empty blue sky

and something in you hurts
in kinda the same way as when
rainclouds hurt before they break open
and you sit down next to him and
look out at your mother's garden

and you want to ask him
if he's ever really going to be happy
or you're supposed to pretend you
don't know that he's going dark
again

and you want to ask him if the
first time he kissed you, he meant it
or he just meant to hurt his future self
because he flinched hard
when you cried in the morning,
nothing sets you off like
how you want him but he'd never let
anything real happen

and you want to ask if maybe
when he was born he cried so loud
he woke the dead and now

a ghost lives with him in his
brainstem

you want to ask if maybe the problem
is really that he doesn't feel anything
much less love
or it's actually just that
you're not good enough

this boy is a spinning top and
a bad choice wrapped up in one, a sense
of disaster in the trail behind him.
he makes you feel exactly the same way
as when you were seven and at the top of a hill
on your brother's bike and halfway down
the brakes stopped working

but you sit there and your tongue is tied
and he's so incredibly insolvably sad inside and
even if it's more than a friendship
but less than dating at least it's something
so even though you want to speak

you say
nothing.

"It's sad he never saw himself the way I saw him. I loved him. I really loved him."

you are fourteen when you discover that girls are a concoction so full of magic that being around them makes your hands shake

at sixteen you kiss your best friend at a party. your fingers find the side of her face, the smooth moon of her jaw, her thick black hair. she tastes like whiskey and your heart hammers against your ribs. she breaks apart from you, laughing, and goes to make out with her boyfriend.

at eighteen you are in a short tight skirt and your eyes are on a golden girl who smells like daisies and never stops smiling and there are six boys around you and they're all begging you to reach for each other and you refuse at first but after four shots suddenly it's all heat and hands and holding her against you, it's the way she feels when she sighs against your lips and how her teeth feel against your neck, it's knowing you messed up hard this time because

you want to kiss her awake in the mornings you want to kiss her over tea you want to kiss her until her toes curl and she forgets how to speak

but she just finds a boy and leaves.

"I like girls but my parents can't know."

I thought I lost you because they buried you under six feet of soil. I remember standing there with my heels sinking into the ground and thinking about how you would have felt claustrophobic. I wanted to dig you up and pour my own life into you because the idea of going on without you felt like a real sad joke told at a wake: nobody really laughs but everyone does their best to smile anyway.

I thought I lost you so I did worse things to myself than you would have been proud of. I think maybe I just wanted to feel something other than that dull ache, you know? It felt like maybe instead of a graveyard, they had torn a hole in my soul. You just weren't there anymore. You weren't there when the grades started slipping, you weren't there for the missed classes, you weren't there for the friends who were more like bullies, you weren't there to stop me from taking that ninth tequila shot, you weren't there to hold my hair back, you weren't there to take me home on the nights I was too sad to party but too weak to say no, you weren't there with your familiar warmth and the curve of your smile. You were just gone.

I didn't find you until two years later when a little girl fell down and her knee bled across her shin and she said, "Don't be sad, stuff like this happens." I didn't find you until I watched little baby birds peck their way into this life. I didn't find you until I was sober and tired and ready to go home when I found a girl passed out on the sofa, too drunk to stand up. I got her showered and warmed up and back to her room and she looked at me and said, "I'm a stranger, why would you help me?" and I felt you right beside me for once in forever and I said, "
Because I can."

We don't die, we pass on. We pass on. Your smile lives in the sunrise and your heartbeat pounds in good music. If I rap against a guitar, I can hear the crack of your knuckles. You're the reason I am strong and kind and patient because you're the one who taught me to be that way. You're in the grass and in the wind and every time I see something beautiful, I find you in it.

I miss you more than poets could make sound pretty. But I'm gonna keep living so your story continues, no matter how bad the pain gets. I'm gonna pass this heart you gave me to every person I meet on the street. I'm gonna give them what you gave me. I'm gonna do my best to make them happy.

This is the closest I can give you to eternity.

"He killed himself."

the sky tonight is the same color as the center of your eye and i miss you.

sometimes they paint waiting as an easy twist of fate, a lover's burden.

they don't speak of the nights full of uncertainty, full of trying to write your name over and over again, full of forgetting exactly what you felt like beside me. they don't speak of how arguments sound over the airwaves, how they tremble and threaten to destroy everything. how it's almost always easier for other people, how romantic places become painful, how watching your friends fall in love becomes awful. they don't speak about the uncertainty, about the hours that stretch without communication, about the pain of knowing that, no matter how desperately you want to, you cannot share every instant

but it is worth it. it always is. every time i lose faith, i look at the night sky again.
i am waiting.

i am waiting.

"For when the distance is too much."

i know very few things about myself, but i know this: the way laughter feels after crying is the absolute best.

i know many facts about animals but the most important is that if you take one away from our ecosystem, they all suffer.

i know so little about the lives of the people i pass. but if there is one thing i understand about us: it is that no matter how often we are broken, the quiet and genuine kindness of humankind leaks out, in every situation. we give with no hope of being paid back, we defend our family with our own bodies, we act in small gentle ways that will never be noticed and never be thanked.

i know this: i have met more than my fair share of people who are filled with bottled rage. but each is far outweighed by people who are good, who are filled with hope: it is simply that they are the softer ones.

so yes, hate speaks loudly. it always does. but a firework is not a volcano, and love is the whole core of earth. hate cannot hope to conquer us.

we are kind to a fault, we write poetry to help others, we tell our stories so others feel less alone, we face our darkness with dance, with art, with song.

there are some things that try to kill us.

and yet

we hold on.

"The power of love is stronger than the power of hate."

ACKNOWLEDGEMENTS

There are a great number of people I should thank for making *Compass* come to life. My family's endless support of my writing, my friends willingly subjected to infinite poetry sessions, every person who calmly put up with my obsession.

And of course, to each of the people who submitted a secret to a poet, who trusted me with a little bit of their life: without you, none of this would have been possible, and I am truly and deeply honored you chose me to tell your story to.

Printed in Great Britain
by Amazon

29497309R00130